D1142386

THE PRINCIPLES OF STATE
INTERFERENCE

THE PRINCIPLES OF STATE INTERFERENCE

*FOUR ESSAYS ON THE POLITICAL PHILOSOPHY
OF MR. HERBERT SPENCER, J. S. MILL,
AND T. H. GREEN*

BY

DAVID G. RITCHIE

Select Bibliographies Reprint Series

 BOOKS FOR LIBRARIES PRESS
FREEPORT, NEW YORK

First Published 1902
Reprinted 1969

STANDARD BOOK NUMBER:
8369-5060-7

LIBRARY OF CONGRESS CATALOG CARD NUMBER:
70-94282

PRINTED IN THE UNITED STATES OF AMERICA

PREFACE.

THE first three essays in this volume were published five years ago in *Time*, and are mainly occupied with a criticism of Mr. Herbert Spencer's *The Man versus the State* and of certain parts of J. S. Mill's *Liberty*. The fourth essay appeared in the *Contemporary Review* for June, 1887. The questions discussed have certainly not declined in importance since these dates. The first three essays have, in parts, undergone considerable alteration. But I have retained the original form and manner of treatment, in the belief that a short and controversial examination of two very well known books may, for many purposes, be more profitable than an elaborate and systematic treatise, for which in any case I have not found the leisure. Something may still be said for using the "dialectical" rather than the "apodeictic" method in political philosophy. And what appears negative criticism does not necessarily give a negative result, least of all when it is criticism of negative criticism. The fourth essay enables me to approach my conclusions in a different manner from that followed in the other three. I have added an Appendix dealing with three questions that seemed to require rather fuller treatment than was possible in footnotes.

January, 1891.

POSTSCRIPT.

THE proofs of this little book had left my hands before the publication of the volume of essays, called *A Plea for Liberty*, for which Mr. Herbert Spencer has written an "Introduction." I have, however, found nothing in that volume which would make it necessary for me to alter any of my arguments. Moreover, the various writers themselves do so much to weaken each other's positions, that they render detailed criticism almost superfluous.

D. G. R.

February, 1891.

THIS Third Edition is a reprint of the first, with no material alteration.

D. G. R.

February, 1902.

CONTENTS.

I.

MR. HERBERT SPENCER'S INDIVIDUALISM, AND HIS CONCEPTION OF SOCIETY.

§ 1. INTRODUCTORY.

MR. SPENCER'S little book, *The Man versus the State*, is the most conspicuous work of recent years in defence of "individualism" and in opposition to the growing tendency of State intervention in matters which the older English economists and Radical politicians held to be best left to private enterprise and unchecked competition. From its very nature it demands and challenges critical examination. Mr. Spencer's conception of what the State is appears to me to involve grave philosophical errors, and to be inconsistent with principles which he himself has done more than any one else to popularise. His practical conclusions, coming with the weight of his authority, seem to require refutation on the part of those who seriously believe that Liberal, or at least Radical, politicians are now moving, however slowly, in the right direction. Mr. Spencer is perhaps the most formidable intellectual foe with whom the New Radicalism has to reckon.

A strong conviction on these points must excuse

the following pages, which might otherwise appear
unduly disrespectful to an honoured name.   No
one who has any interest in philosophy can refuse
admiration to an Englishman who has given the
energies of his life to philosophical studies, who
believes that philosophy must be systematic, and
who, although acting up to this belief, has made his
countrymen read his books.   But there are some
things that demand more respect than distinguished
persons—philosophy itself, and the growing sense of
a common and public responsibility to diminish the
misery of human life.

§ 2. ARE RADICALS TORIES?

"*Laissez faire*" and " Freedom of Contract " used
to be Liberal watchwords, but have now been given
up or left to the Tories. Mr. Spencer suggests the
easy explanation, that the Liberals have mistakenly
adopted the Tory policy.   English political parties
have a long history and a very complex significance.
But to our synthetic philosopher, who deals in " completely unified knowledge," this is all very simple.
There are, according to Mr. Spencer, two great types
of society, the militant and the industrial (an idea
which may be found in Comte).   To the former
belongs the *régime* of *status,* to the latter that of

contract (this comes from Sir Henry Maine). The
former adopts compulsory co-operation, the latter
voluntary co-operation (this, I believe, is Mr. Spencer's own invention).   Now the Tories are the party
who hold by the former or worn-out type of society ;
the Liberals, by the latter.   So that when a Liberal
is found attacking what is called " the freedom of
contract," he must, in order to make Mr. Spencer's
completely unified knowledge correct, be no longer a
Liberal, but a " New Tory." [1]   How is it then, that
Liberals and Tories have come to change places
in relation to the question of State interference ?
According to Mr. Spencer, the essence of Liberal
efforts has been the struggle for individualism against
Governments—not against bad or despotic Governments merely, but against Governments as such.
" The abolition of grievances suffered by the people,"
" the gaining of a popular good," has been merely an
"external conspicuous trait." [2]   People in general have
made a mistake in classification, and taken the external trait for the important thing.   " The popular
good has come to be sought by Liberals, not as an
end to be indirectly gained by relaxation of re-

[1] *The Man versus the State*, pp. 1 ff.
[2] *Ibid.*, p. 7.

straints, but as an end to be directly gained." There is a philosophical difficulty here which needs to be cleared up. I do not see why, because an end is sometimes indirectly pursued, it ceases to be an end, and becomes merely "an external conspicuous trait." Least of all do I see how Mr. Spencer can logically hold such a position. He considers pleasure to be the ultimate end of conduct ; and yet I suppose he would allow, like Mill, that it is an end which can only be gained by not being directly pursued. I should be very ready to admit that pleasure is "an external conspicuous trait," which Mr. Spencer and others have mistaken for the end—a conclusion which would seem to follow, if Mr. Spencer's argument here is correct. The ultimate end of all human effort may be indirectly pursued, and the popular, or rather the common, good is this end, while pleasure is not.

But let us leave this philosophical question for the present. The unsophisticated mind is certainly a little surprised to learn that the welfare of the people is only "an external trait." I had always thought that, when men fought for liberty, and checked the tyranny of kings and potentates, they did it for the sake of the common weal, and not for the sake of carrying out Mr. Spencer's theory about the nega-tively regulative function of the State.   Sometimes

the common welfare has been promoted by resisting
and restraining bad interference, sometimes by insti-
tuting Government action to check evils that have
grown up through past bad interference or through
long-continued neglect. There is a time to break
down and a time to build up ; and the same men
may have to do both. If Mr. Spencer came one
day on a company of workmen demolishing a large
building, and some days afterwards found them
erecting something else on the same place, he would
say to them : " You have mistaken your work. Your
business is to make the way clear for individuals like
myself to walk about in as we choose." Some one
might perhaps answer him : " The other day we were
pulling down an old palace and an old prison; to-day
we are building a school and a library." There is
no necessary inconsistency in the same party having
struggled against protection, monopolies, and privileges, which favoured a few individuals at the cost
of the vast mass of the people, and now struggling
to protect individuals who are not wise enough nor
strong enough to protect themselves against the
selfishness of those whom past legislation, or past
neglect, has allowed to acquire an undue power over
them. At the same time there does, on the surface,
appear to be a certain inconsistency; and this appear-

ance deters many from lending a helping hand in
the cause which they really have at heart. Those
who abolished the Corn Laws kicked at first vehe-
mently against the Factory Acts. The view that the
main work of Liberalism is to diminish the amount
of Government action is still widely spread in this
country. It is a view which seems to fit in extremely
well with the ideas, or at least with the language,
of the average Englishman. Of this we may find
several explanations.

In a country where political freedom has been won,
not by a sudden revolution transferring power from
one class to another, but by a very long and very
gradual series of struggles between the non-privileged
and the privileged, or between the more privileged
and the less privileged classes, this long struggle has
left as an inheritance a permanent jealousy of rulers,
a ready-made disposition to suspect and resent
Government interference. The struggle against the
arbitrary rule of the Stuarts has made an indelible
impression on English political thinking. This we
may call the Whig tradition, in which we include the
Puritan tradition. The best of the Puritans fought
for the liberty of individual conscience ; and nearly
all of them, when they could not have their own way,
wished to be left alone in matters of religion.

Secondly, besides this older Whig tradition, there is the more recent tradition from the struggles of the present century—the long fight against State interference, especially with trade, but also with freedom of the press, of religious belief, of association, etc. The struggle of the seventeenth century was mainly against unconstitutional and arbitrary kinds of Government. That of the first half of this century has been against mischievous kinds of Government action. The opponents of some particular kind of bad Government interference often used the unnecessarily wide premiss, "All Government interference is bad." The advocates of free trade tended to apply the phrase *Laissez faire* in all matters. It became the dogma of the old-fashioned Radical.[1]

Thirdly, there is the patriotic feeling that we are not as other men are, the national pride in the English system of leaving people to do things for themselves, and the prejudice against everything that any one can call "continental bureaucracy." Now most undoubtedly we have a great gain, not in the

---

[1] Cp. an article in *The Times* of Feb. 15th, 1883, quoted by Lord Pembroke in his pamphlet, *Liberty and Socialism*, p. 29, according to which "one of the chief notes of instructed Liberalism was [a generation ago] the dogma, that the best Government is that which interferes least with social affairs."

mere absence of Government action, but in the habit
of free association ; many of the advantages however
that we are apt to ascribe to absence of Government
interference are really due to the absence of centra-
lisation—a very different thing.   A highly differentiated and decentralised Government is not identical
with no Government at all.[1]   French and German
writers often talk with admiration of our "self-
government," and we may feel flattered by the fact
that they have borrowed our word.   But we know
in our inmost hearts how defective our local government is (even in spite of recent legislation), how
chaotic its condition, how much more of it we need,
and how much more controlled it often requires to
be.   Many good measures are nearly inoperative
through the remissness of local bodies.   On the
other hand, the central Government labours under the
burden of local details ; and much decentralisation is
urgently needed.

---

[1] Cp. Sir F. Pollock, *History of the Science of Politics* (London, 1890), p. 123 : "The minimisers [of the State's function]
appear not to distinguish sufficiently the action of the State in
general from its centralised action.   There are many things
which the State cannot do in the way of central government, or
not effectually, but which can be very well done by the action
of local governing bodies.   But this is a question between the
direct and the delegated activity of the State, not between State
action and individual enterprise."

Underlying all these traditions and prejudices there is a particular metaphysical theory—a metaphysical theory which takes hold of those persons especially who are fondest of abjuring all metaphysics ; and the disease is in their case the more dangerous since they do not know when they have it. The chief symptom of this metaphysical complaint is the belief in the abstract individual. The individual is thought of, at least spoken of, as if he had a meaning and significance apart from his surroundings and apart from his relations to the community of which he is a member. It may be quite true that the significance of the individual is not exhausted by his relations to any given set of surroundings ; but apart from all of these he is a mere abstraction—a logical ghost, a metaphysical spectre, which haunts the habitations of those who have derided metaphysics. The individual, apart from all relations to a community, is a negation. You can say nothing about him, or rather it, except that it is not any other individual.[2] Now, along with this negative and abstract view of the individual there goes, as counterpart, the way of

---

[2] Cp. Mr. Montague's admirable exposure of " the plump and solid individual " of our ordinary phraseology in his *Limits of Individual Liberty*, pp. 55 ff.

looking at the State as an opposing element to the individual. The individual and the State are put over against one another. Their relation is regarded as one merely of antithesis. Of course, this is a point of view which we can take, and quite rightly for certain purposes; but it is only one point of view. It expresses only a partial truth; and a partial truth, if accepted as the whole truth, is always a falsehood. Such a conception is, in any case, quite inadequate as a basis for any profitable discussion of the duties of Government.

It is this theory of the individual which underlies Mill's famous book on *Liberty*. Mill, and all those who take up his attitude toward the State, seem to assume that all power gained by the State is so much taken from the individual; and, conversely, that all power gained by the individual is gained at the expense of the State. Now this is to treat the two elements, power of the State and power (or liberty) of the individual, as if they formed the debit and credit sides of an account book; it is to make them like two heaps of a fixed number of stones, to neither of which can you add without taking from the other. It is to apply a mere quantitative conception in politics, as if that were an adequate "category" in such matters. The same thing is done when society is

spoken of as merely " an aggregate of individuals."
The citizen of a State, the member of a society of any
sort, even an artificial or temporary association, does
not stand in the same relation to the whole that one
number does to a series of numbers, or that one
stone does to a heap of stones.　Even ordinary language shows us this.　We feel it to be a more
adequate expression to say that the citizen is a
member of the body politic, than to call him merely
a unit in a political aggregate.　For certain purposes
of course he is treated merely as a unit.　In the
voting at an election we count heads (" to save the
trouble of breaking them ") ; but a citizen's existence
as such is not exhausted by his voting once in several
years.　Rousseau, carrying out his abstract individualism thoroughly in this respect, said that the
English people were only free at a general election, and in the short moments of their liberty
they made such a bad use of it that they deserved
to lose it.[1]

§ 3.　THE SOCIAL ORGANISM.

" But, surely, all this is beside the question.　Has
not Mr. Spencer told us again and again that society

---

[1] *Contrat Social*, iii. 15.

is an organism ? "   Yes, Mr. Spencer has told us so.
The phrase "social organism" has come to him
from Comte, in what way Mr. F. Harrison and he
may settle between them.   But, if Mr. Spencer had
only given more attention to Comte's writings, he
might have come to believe more in his phrase than
he apparently does.   Let us see what he tells us
about the social organism.   So far as I know, he
has not retracted any part of the essay which he
first published in the *Westminster Review* in 1860,
although, in his *Principles of Sociology*, he has not
repeated everything contained in it.   In this essay
is to be found the famous parallel between the up
and down lines of the railway which supplies the
circulation of commodities in the social organism, and
the arteries and veins of a well-developed animal,
money being the blood corpuscles, and the telegraph
wires the nerves.   If Plato's Socrates had told us
a "myth" of this sort, he would have introduced
it by an apology about his not being very good at
the making of images.   In almost any other modern
writer we might have thought it a *jeu d'esprit.*   But
this supposition is inapplicable in the case of the
author of the system of " Synthetic Philosophy."

There are many difficulties in this conception, of
which we should be very glad to have a solution.

In the first place, it is distressing to find that when society is called an organism, it is not to be compared with any noble animal,[1] such as the lion or the eagle, under which forms we are accustomed to figure a nation, but that it belongs to an extremely low type.   We are "bodies dispersed through an indifferentiated jelly."[2]   This, we suppose, represents the British citizen moving in his national fog.   But

---

[1] Bluntschli is strongly impressed by the organic character of the State ; but he insists that it is human.   Nay, he is even more precise.   The State is not merely *homo* (common gender) it is the man ; the Church being what Homer and Artemus Ward would call "the female woman."   See his *Theory of the State*, English translation, p. 22.

[2] Compare *Principles of Sociology*, p. 475.   "The parts of a society form a whole that is discrete."   It is obvious that Mr. Spencer is really thinking only of the spatially separated individual human *bodies ;* but the individuals who compose a human society are not mere animal organisms capable of movement through space.   The individual *person*, the citizen with rights and duties, is a complex of ideas, emotions, and aspirations which are altogether unintelligible except as the product of ceaseless action and reaction in the spiritual (*i.e.* intellectual, moral, etc.) environment, which not merely surrounds, but actually constitutes the individual—*i.e.* makes him what he is. The history of the individual cannot be understood apart from the history of the race, though of course in practice we have to limit ourselves to a small portion.   We never can understand any individual thing or person fully, just because we cannot grasp the whole universe   How that which is a "complex" and a "product" can yet know itself as a unity, is a problem that psychology and history cannot solve.

afterwards we are glad to find that the social organism is rather like the vertebrate type, but lower than human. So there is some chance for the British lion after all. Or is our society a leviathan, as Hobbes thought, or some quite fabulous beast? Of course it will be answered, "In some respects the social organism is of one sort, in some respects of another." But if the description is to be so ambiguous and wavering, is it not just possible that, "in some respects," the social organism is not like any animal organism whatever?

Again, if society is an organism, the more advanced a community is, the more highly developed should be the organism to which it corresponds. But individual independence within the social organism has to be paralleled by the inferior classes of animals. The analogy of the animal would suggest that in the higher types of the social organism there should be a very great coherence—in fact, a "corporate consciousness"; and this was the conclusion which Plato drew from his, still unformulated, conception of the social organism. "Is not the best-ordered State that which most nearly approaches to the condition of the individual: as in the body, when but a finger is hurt, the whole frame drawn towards the soul, and forming one realm under the ruling power therein, feels the hurt, and sympathises altogether with the part affected, and we say that the man has a pain in his finger ? " (*Rep.* 462.)[1]

Mr. Spencer, however, holds that, "as there is no social sensorium, it results that the welfare of the aggregate, considered apart from that of the units, is not an end to be sought. The society exists for the benefit of its members, not its members for the benefit of the society" (*Principles of Sociology,* p. 479). Is it not his political creed of individualism which leads Mr. Spencer to deny the existence of a social sensorium, and to deny to the social organism the important characteristic of all organisms—the dependence of the parts upon the whole ?

Again, the more advanced community might be expected to correspond to the more highly differentiated organism. Progress, as Mr. Spencer has told us more than once, is from the homogeneous and indefinite to the heterogeneous and definite. Now Mr. Spencer, as politician, would undoubtedly regard the United States of America as more advanced than Germany; but an American citizen may very well be a manufacturer in his industrial aspect, a "colonel" in his militant, a philosopher of Mr.

---

[1] Mr. Spencer, in his *Principles of Sociology,* p. 611, refers to Plato's parallelisms between States and individuals, but does not notice this passage.

Spencer's school, and a legislator, not quite after
Mr. Spencer's heart, all at the same time; so that
to Mr. Spencer, as biological philosopher, America
ought to appear one of those rude organisms which
do not make the delicate distinction between
stomachs and mouths. A highly developed social
organism, if it is to be definite as well as heterogeneous, would really require a caste system—such
as Plato proposed. But a caste system, I suspect,
would not meet the approval of Mr. Spencer as
politician, nor would anything Platonic meet his
approval as philosopher. So here is a difficulty.
The answer again would probably be : that " in some
respects " the social organism resembles one kind of
animal organism, and " in some respects " another ;
which again leads us to a suspicion that in some
respects it is not like any animal organism whatever.

The inconsistency between Mr. Spencer's philosophy and his politics has already been pointed out
by a sympathetic French critic, M. Henri Marion,
whose objections Mr. Spencer seeks to answer in a
" Postscript " added in the edition of 1877 of the
Principles of Sociology (p. 618, *a, b*). In the higher
individual organisms it is admitted that the nervous
system is highly developed and centralised, because
of the needs of the animal in its struggle with nature
and with other animals. In the social organism,

however, Mr. Spencer argues that a highly developed and centralised regulative system is needed in the militant stage, but not in the industrial; the highest type of social organism being that which has "a largely developed sustaining or industrial system with a feeble regulating or governmental system." This reply of Mr. Spencer has, in turn, been completely answered by another sympathetic French critic, M. Fouillée, whose criticism has the value that always belongs to a criticism from within.[1] M. Fouillée quite approves of Mr. Spencer making the nervous system the biological equivalent of government in the social organism. But he points out that in the higher animals a centralised nervous system does not serve for external actions only, such as the catching of prey, but for sensibility, thought, will. And in the social organism it is not true that the industrial *régime* needs only a feeble regulative system : for industrialism requires " the development (1) of sympathy, which leads to association and to the division of labour; (2) of intelligence, which leads to the progress of the sciences and arts ; and (3) of will, which is the liberty of individuals in a solidarity to which they consent." Does not all

---

[1] *La Science Sociale Contemporaine*, pp. 162 ff.

this, asks M. Fouillée, imply a very perfect " nervous system," and not merely an " alimentary " ?

If Mr. Spencer's " Postscript " be carefully examined, it will be found to amount practically to an abdication of the " Social Organism " theory in favour of Utilitarianism, with the assumption that Mr. Spencer knows what the highest type of society is, quite apart from any help to be derived from biology. " Social organisation," he says, "is to be considered high in proportion as it subserves individual welfare, because in a society the units are sentient and the aggregate insentient ; and the industrial type is higher because it subserves individual welfare better than the militant type." As to that, strange as it may seem to Mr. Spencer, there may possibly be two opinions. The militant type, it may be urged, at least mitigates the struggle for existence within each united society ; the industrial type, in Mr. Spencer's extreme form of it, restores that unmitigated struggle beween individuals, in which the unsuccessful perish, not quickly by the sword, but slowly by starvation.

But—to return to the social organism—we are delighted to learn from Mr. Spencer that the Houses of Parliament (not excluding the House of Peers) resemble the cerebral masses in a vertebrate animal.

Now, one would have thought that a vertebrate animal with cerebral masses was superior to those individuals that moved about in an indifferentiated jelly; but, considering all the uncomplimentary things Mr. Spencer says about our legislators, we are led to have dreadful suspicions as to the species of animal to whose cerebral masses they correspond; or else, "in some respects," apparently, they are not like cerebral masses at all : and we conclude that Mr. Spencer (like Professor Drummond, who has found all the dogmas of Calvin in the System of Synthetic Philosophy) has mistaken an ingenious illustration for a scientific fact.

It might be said that this last objection is sufficiently met by the answer given in *Essays*, vol. iii., pp. 6, 7, to Professor Huxley ; but we cannot see what justifies Mr. Spencer (except an intelligible desire to make his theories fit together) in arbitrarily comparing the negatively regulative functions of Government with those of the cerebro-spinal nervous system, and leaving everything else for the visceral nervous system. Apparently the social organism in Mr. Spencer's ideal State, where Government is no longer needed, ought to resemble an animal drunk or asleep, with the brain doing as little as possible (p. 8).

Thus, from the doctrine of the social organism, as expounded by Mr. Spencer, we find it difficult to arrive at any coherent theory of politics. In fact, the conception of society as an organism seems to admit of more easy applications to the defence of just those very views about the State which Mr. Spencer most dislikes; and, though the conception of organism has its value in helping political thinking out of the confusions of individualism, if it be taken as the final key to all mysteries, it leads to new confusions of its own, for which it would be absurd to blame Mr. Spencer.

§ 4. INDIVIDUALISM.

But not only do we find Mr. Spencer's politics defective because he takes the idea of organism as final, but because he does not really get as much out of the idea as he might. In spite of the constant parade of biological illustration, it would appear that in his political thinking Mr. Spencer has not advanced beyond the arithmetical and mechanical conceptions of society which prevailed in the days when it was still a striking thing to say, "Constitutions are not made, but grow." Society, to Mr. Spencer, is only an aggregate of individuals. The individuals are assumed, to start with. They are put together, and society is made ; and Mr. Spencer criticises the mode of its making. He has not got beyond Hobbes.

Of course, this charge will be indignantly denied. But the proof of it is staring us in the face : *The Man VERSUS the State.* In the very title of these essays, and throughout, it is assumed, as much as by Mill, that every increase of the powers of Government (Mr. Spencer uses " Government " and " State " as convertible terms [1]) implies an equivalent decrease in the liberties of individuals. Now, this is a way of speaking which produces accurate-looking, quasi-scientific, abstractly logical expressions ; but it is profoundly "inorganic." An organism is not an

---

[1] They are certainly often so used in ordinary language ; but it is a pity not to take the terms in a more precise sense. Let us call *society organised* the *State.* The *Constitution* is the organisation as distinguishable in thought from the society. *Government* is either equivalent to *Constitution* (as when we talk of different forms of government), or is used specially for the administrative or executive element in the State ; *i.e.* for what appears specially as the head, or ruling part, of the State. Thus, of course, when the State *acts*, the Government acts, and *vice versâ* ; and so the words come to be interchanged. Where the Germans say *Staat*, we frequently use " nation," in a somewhat more definite sense than their *Volk*. Our word "people," again, is often the same as the German *Volk*, or Latin *populus*, and more precise than the German *Nation*. See Note A, "On the Distinction between Society and the State."

equation. In a healthy body—I must beg Mr. Spencer's pardon for using smaller words than seem to be proper in the mouths of those who deal with "completely unified knowledge"—in a healthy body all the parts may develop together. Because a man has strong arms, he has not *therefore* weak legs. Unfortunately, brain and muscle do not always grow together; but this we regard as an imperfection. Now, if society is an organism, a State in which the powers of Government are abnormally large might be like a body with a brain overgrown at the expense of sinew and flesh (though, indeed, if Mr. Spencer be right in classing such States under the species militant, the muscular beast of prey might seem the better analogue); but a perfectly healthy, well-developed society ought to resemble a body in which well-developed brain and well-developed limb go together and help each other. If this is not so, then it ought to follow that society is not an organism, which, according to Mr. Spencer, is absurd; and yet it is Mr. Spencer himself who contradicts the possibility of Government and individual gaining in strength together.

A sentence from the essay on "The Sins of Legislators" will supply a further proof of the mechanical, or rather the merely arithmetical, character of Mr.

Spencer's political thinking. "Social activities," we are there told, "are the aggregate results of the desires of individuals who are severally seeking satisfaction" (p. 62). Nay, even in the very Essay on the Social Organism, Mr. Spencer speaks of the office of Parliament as that of "*averaging* the interests of the various classes in the community," as the brain "*averages* the interests of life." If this remark is to be taken seriously, there ought to be a science of political arithmetic, parallel I suppose to the calculus of pleasure. But such a mode of speaking and thinking about society would imply that the acts of a combination of individuals are the same as a combination of the acts done by the same individuals, a supposition which is not true even of voluntary, temporary and artificial associations. A society of one hundred individuals for the promotion of a particular end is something more than the aggregate of a hundred individuals working independently towards this same end. But, even according to Mr. Spencer, the State does not arise from a voluntary combination as on Hobbes' theory; and it certainly is not a temporary combination. Therefore, *à fortiori*, this arithmetic cannot apply to the State. Least of all can it do so if society is an organism.

But apart from the question of logical consistency,

let us consider the more important question of truth.
Is it true, as a fact, that as Government gains in
strength, the individual loses in freedom and *vice
versâ?* Now Mr. Spencer would admit that the individual is more free under the modern than under
the mediæval State ; but is this because the modern
State is less powerful ? The opposite is decidedly
true.   As Sir J. Fitzjames Stephen says : " The
difference between a rough and a civilised society
is not that force is used in the one case and per-
suasion in the other, but that force is (or ought to be)
guided with greater care in the second case than in
the first.   President Lincoln attained his objects by
the use of a degree of force which would have
crushed Charlemagne and his paladins and peers like
so many eggshells." [1]   To take a quite clear test,
contrast the savage or barbarian with the civilised
man.   " The modern English citizen who lives under
the burden of the revised edition of the Statutes, not

---

[1] *Liberty, Equality, Fraternity*, p. 32 (Edit. 2).   May an ac-
knowledgment be made here, once for all, of the debt we owe
to Sir J. Fitzjames Stephen's vigorous book ?—a debt which
may be freely acknowledged by those who dissent entirely from
his conclusions.   The purely legal mind cannot deal satisfac-
torily with the problems of history and politics ; but the purely
legal mind sees perfectly clearly within definite and easily
recognisable limits.

to speak of innumerable municipal, railroad, sanitary, and other bye-laws, is, after all, an infinitely freer as well as nobler creature than the savage who is always under the despotism of physical want."[1] Thus Professor Jevons. So too Spinoza : " Homo, qui ratione ducitur, magis in civitate, ubi ex communi decreto vivit, quam in solitudine, ubi sibi soli obtemperat, liber est." Bagehot, whom Mr. Spencer would probably regard as a better authority than Spinoza, and who has admirably shown in his *Physics and Politics* how biological conceptions may be applied to the study of human society without distorting the historical judgment, has insisted in his *Economic Studies* that the individual freedom, which the old school of English economists assume, " presupposes the pervading intervention of an effectual Government—the last triumph of civilisation, and one to which early times had nothing comparable."[2] These sayings are not quoted to prove the point by a consensus of authorities, but only as striking ways in which a lesson of history has been expressed. Of course it is a lesson of history which Mr. Spencer does not

---

[1] Professor Jevons, *The State in Relation to Labour*, pp. 14, 15.
[2] *The Postulates of English Political Economy*, p. 48.

believe.   It is not written in the folios of *Descriptive Sociology.*

Mr. Spencer might, however, still answer: "I do allow Government in an advanced stage of society a sphere of activity; that, namely, of being negatively regulative."   That sphere however is much less than what the facts of historical progress show.   Mr. Spencer makes progress imply a "restriction and limitation of State functions."   He finds fault with Austin for "assimilating civil authority to military,"[1] by which he appears to mean that State authority ought now to be less than it was in the militant stage of society, in which stage he would certainly place the Middle Ages.

During the Middle Ages the conception of the nation was indistinct, and the power of the central authority was feeble; but was the individual proportionately free?   Far from it; feudal barons and ecclesiastical and trading corporations were strong against him.   Custom was omnipotent.   Law had little force.   The break up of feudalism is everywhere characterised by the rise of distinctly marked nations governed by absolute kings.   In many respects there was loss, especially where the absolute power of the

---

[1] *The Man versus the State*, p. 81.

monarch lasted a long time, as in France ; but it was the absolutism of the Tudors which finally made the commons of England strong against the privileged orders of clergy and nobility, and it was the absolutism of Louis XI. and of Louis XIV. which finally caused the ruin of the old *régime* in France. The fact that absolutism in government and individualism in sentiment coincide, alike in the Roman empire and at the Reformation, would be quite inexplicable according to the theory of society which Mr. Spencer adopts when he is dealing with practical politics. To a really " organic " conception of society, the coincidence is a necessary one.

As has been already said, Mr. Spencer, neglecting the organic nature of society, assumes, in explaining its origin and growth, that he has the individual to start with. The physical individual, of course, is there ; but not the individual whose rights and liberties Mr. Spencer is so anxious to protect against the aggression of governments. In primitive societies the *person* does not exist, or exists only potentially, or, as we might say, *in spe*. The person is the product of the State. Mr. Spencer is presumably acquainted with the writings of Sir Henry Maine. He has adopted the formula " from status to contract." Two of Maine's works are named in the list of authorities at the end of *Political Institutions*; not however the *Ancient Law*, in which[1] occur the words whose truth is confirmed by all we can learn about early society. " The unit of an ancient society was the family, of a modern society the individual."   The doctrine is summed up (in the index) in the words : " Society in primitive times not a collection of individuals, but an aggregation of families."   This remains true on the whole, even if we are to suppose, with McLennan and many other anthropologists, that a looser and vaguer form of common life universally preceded the *patriarchal* family.   Primitive property was everywhere communal (whatever the community might be), not personal.   Now the astonishing thing is this : a recognition of the fact that definite heterogeneous individuals—*i.e. persons* with definite rights—are only gradually developed out of the homogeneous undifferentiated mass of primitive society would have fitted in admirably with Mr. Spencer's biological theory of progress and of the social organism.   But, unfortunately, it does not fit in with his political superstition about the natural rights of the individual, which we shall presently have to consider.   More-

---

[1] Page 126.

over, such a formula of the development of the individual would require to be supplemented by a recognition of the part taken by Governments in his development; and for this we fear biological conceptions are inadequate. The person is not a mere natural product ; in part he is created by the *conscious* work of law and religion. The Roman jurists and the Christian teaching of several centuries have a share in the differentiation of the individual from his social environment. It is the function of the modern State to carry on this work.

§ 5. NATURAL RIGHTS.

If further proof were required that Mr. Spencer's actual political thinking is of the same kind as that of Mill, who was unaffected by the conceptions of organism and evolution, it may be found in such passages as those in which Mr. Spencer speaks of the *proper* function of Government being the maintenance of social order (*The Man versus the State*, p. 63) ; or, again, of a private *sphere* into which the State "has decreased its intrusions" (*ibid.*, p. 94). Nay, we need not look for anything underlying. On the surface comes up, in an essay on political superstitions by the author of the great system of evolutionary philosophy, a theory of natural rights.

Verily, the eighteenth century is avenged. And for
proof of this theory of natural rights ? First of all,
a shy reference to the German doctrine of *Naturrecht.*
" One might have expected that utterances to this
effect " (he has just quoted Professor Jevons and Mr.
Matthew Arnold) " would have been rendered less
dogmatic by the knowledge that a whole school of
legists on the Continent maintains a belief diametrically opposed to that maintained by the English
school. The idea of *Naturrecht* is the root-idea of
German jurisprudence. Now, whatever, may be the
opinion held respecting German philosophy at large,
it ['it' must be understood as referring to 'philosophy,' not to 'opinion'] cannot be characterised as
shallow. A doctrine current among a people distinguished above all others as laborious inquirers,
and certainly not to be classed with superficial
thinkers, should not be dismissed as though it were
nothing more than a popular delusion." [1] This is a
delightful passage. Suppose we were to imitate it
as follows : " One might have expected that utterances about the folly of trusting Governments would
have been rendered less dogmatic by the knowledge
that a whole school of political philosophers on the

---

[1] *The Man versus the State*, p. 87.

Continent maintains a belief diametrically opposed to that maintained by the English school. The idea of State action is the root-idea of German political philosophy"; and so on as before. Of course those who know what *Naturrecht* means know that it does not mean, and cannot be correctly translated by the term, "natural *rights.*" But probably Mr. Spencer is not aware of this, as his studies have not led him far in the direction of German philosophy. Sir F. Pollock has rightly pointed out that *Naturrecht* is much the same sort of thing as Bentham's theory of legislation.[1] It is an ideal code, "purporting to be justified by the universal nature of human relations, and qualified by no respect of time or place."

Secondly, there is a most edifying criticism of Bentham's statement that "Government creates rights."[2] This Mr. Spencer thinks might be intelligible, if it came from an absolutist like Hobbes or the king of Dahomey, but he cannot understand how Bentham holds it along with the view that the largest possible portion of the people should have the sovereign power. "Mark now what happens when we put these two doctrines together. The

---

[1] *Hist. of the Science of Politics,* pp. 109–112.
[2] *The Man versus the State,* pp. 88, 89.

sovereign people jointly appoint representatives, and
so create a Government; the Government thus
created creates rights; and then, having created
rights, it confers them on the separate members of
the sovereign people by which it was itself created.
Here is a marvellous piece of political legerdemain!
Mr. Matthew Arnold, contending that 'property is
the creator of the law,' tells us to beware of the
'metaphysical phantom of property in itself.' Surely,
among metaphysical phantoms the most shadowy is
this which supposes [1] a thing to be obtained by
creating an agent, which creates the thing, and then
confers the thing on its own creator." In this
passage let us note that "a right" is talked of as "a
thing," to which therefore the saying, *Ex nihilo nihil
fit*, will apply. Yet there is really no "legerdemain."
Suppose a company of persons meet together for
the purpose of founding a society—let us say for
the study of Mr. Spencer's System of Synthetic Philosophy. They appoint a committee to draw up rules.
These rules are accepted by a vote of all the units
(or by a majority, to which the minority voluntarily
give way). The individuals, as members of the

---

[1] Does Mr. Spencer mean that Matthew Arnold is "a meta
physical phantom"?   It is he that "supposes."

society, have now rights (and of course duties) which they did not have before : *e.g.* they have to pay subscriptions, they may write after their names M.S.S.S.S.P., and they may have the crystal-plant-grub-butterfly emblem stamped on their note-paper. The trick is done. A right is created out of nothing.[1] Now I am not prepared to defend the political philosophy of Jeremy Bentham out and out ; but I am ready, were there any need, to take up the cudgels for him and Matthew Arnold (who, by the way, seems in queer company) against this particular accusation of juggling.

After this quaint invocation of the wisdom of the Germans and this edifying assault on the metaphysics of Bentham come the positive proofs which Mr. Spencer advances for the existence of natural rights. There is, first of all, the statement that "before definite government arises, conduct is regulated by customs."[2] This not very startling remark is proved by an

---

[1] "Nothing is more real than a right, yet its existence is purely ideal" ; *i.e.* "has its being solely in consciousness" (T. H. Green, *Philosophical Works*, ii., p. 446). Green holds that society makes rights, which exist antecedently to the State ; but then he limits the application of the term "State" to a social stage, like that of the Greek city-state or the modern nation ; *i.e.* he uses "State" only for the developed State.

[2] *The Man versus the State*, pp. 90 ff.

appeal to the Bechuanas, the Koranna Hottentots, the Araucanians, the Kirghizes, the Dyaks, the people of Madagascar, Java, Sumatra, Ashantee, the Chippewayans, Ahts, Comanchees, Esquimaux, the Brazilian Indians, the Todas, and the "peaceful Arafuras." It is a pity that Mr. Spencer did not also refer to a certain obscure people who called themselves Hellenes, who have not yet been cut up into tables of descriptive sociology, and to a certain unsystematic sociologist called Herodotus, who quotes a certain unscientific writer called Pindar, who said that "custom is king of all men." Suppose we admit that even very rude races do recognise a right, say, of property, basing that right solely on custom, what does this prove? It proves certainly that all rights cannot arise in an explicit contract or through a statute made by a definite legislature; but does it prove that rights are antecedent to and independent of the acts of society? If Mr. Spencer had thought the Greek writer above referred to worthy of his attention, he might have learnt that the same word in Greek signifies "custom" and "law," a linguistic confirmation of the view of Sir Henry Maine, that all primitive law is a declaration of custom, and not a command (as Austin thought). The conception of command is very much later; and it is only when society has far advanced that laws consciously and deliberately made come in to check customs which have grown up. But these customs were not always there ; they are the products—we may perfectly well say the creations—of society. There was no need to go to the Todas and the peaceful Arafuras—and the blameless Ethiopians—to find rights growing up out of customs. It has been observed by competent scientific inquirers that even in recent times English schoolboys have claimed a customary right to share in the plum-cake which another boy receives from his fond mother. Nay, the boy who dares to violate the most senseless or even mischievous school tradition has often a hard time of it. Surely Mr. Spencer would not call these things "natural rights" ; or is it only among *old* barbarians that "natural rights" can be observed ?

"Property," says Mr. Spencer, "was well recognised before law existed." Yes, I answer ; but the customs of a primitive society are its laws, and, as the product of society, vary in different societies. By right of property, which Mr. Spencer considers a natural right, he clearly means an absolute and individual right, which he thinks the State ought to protect, but ought not to interfere with. But the rights of property, as they generally exist among primitive peoples, are not rights of individual property at all. Property belongs to the family, the village, the tribe. In Mr. Spencer's *Political Institutions*, chapter xv., it is very well shown how at first the ideas of property are very vague, and how the idea of property in anything except movables (including captives in war) is unknown. Now, under rights of property our Tory defenders of "freedom of contract," of whom Mr. Spencer seems to approve, most certainly include property in land. But Mr. Spencer's appeal to natural rights would not defend from State interference property in land, and yet it would defend property in slaves ! In deciding what form of land tenure is most advantageous for the welfare of the community and of individuals, we can get no help whatever from any revelation of "natural rights."

Next comes a familiar old argument which has seen service in many an "intuitionist" refutation of empiricism. There is an approach to uniformity in the rights which different Governments recognise. Therefore, it is argued, there must be some "determining cause over-ruling their decisions."[1] But the reason is not "natural rights," in any sense in which

---

[1] *The Man versus the State*, p. 92.

this doctrine contradicts the statement that society creates rights. It is simply this : there are certain conditions necessary to the life of any society. In order to hold together, every society formally, or informally, agrees to observe, or, let us say, finds itself compelled to observe, these conditions of common life, and thereby creates rights and duties for its members. Now, Mr. Spencer himself really says the same thing, giving it as the ultimate "secret." He traces "natural rights" back to the general conditions of social life.[1] Here he has got on his own ground again, and most of what is said is unexceptionable. " Clearly the conception of 'natural rights' originates in the recognition of the truth, that if life is justifiable, there must be a justification for the performance of acts essential to its preservation ; and, therefore, a justification for those liberties and claims which make such acts possible." [2]

The third "historical evidence" is a full recognition of what we have been urging ; namely, that "as social organisation advances, the central ruling power undertakes more and more to secure to individuals their personal safety, the safety of their possessions, and,

---

[1] *The Man versus the State*, p. 95.
[2] *Ibid.*, p. 96.

to some extent, the enforcement of their claims established by contract.   Originally concerned almost
exclusively with defence of the society as a whole
against other societies, or with conducting its attacks
on other societies, Government has come more and
more to discharge the function of defending individuals against each other." [1] Now, this passage seems
to me to contain a recognition of the truths, (1) that
society does not begin with " persons," but produces
them ; (2) that the " person" is produced by Government increasing its functions.   I hardly see how it
is consistent with Mr. Spencer's practical thesis, that
the power of Governments ought to diminish ; still
less how it proves that thesis or any part of it.   Can
Mr. Spencer really mean that all the personal rights
which the British Government secures to its citizens
always existed as " natural rights " ?   Probably Mr.
Spencer regards some sort of copyright as necessary
to secure to him that justice which he has defined as
"a rigorous maintenance of those normal relations
among citizens under which each gets in return for his
labour, skilled or unskilled, bodily or mental, as much
as is proved to be its value by the demand for it ;
such return therefore as will enable him to thrive

---

[1] *The Man versus the State*, p. 93.

and rear offspring in proportion to the superiorities which make him valuable to himself and others."[1] But did the Todas or the peaceful Arafuras—to say nothing of the by no means peaceful Angles and Saxons—recognise copyright ? On the other hand, most races have at some time or other recognised a "natural right" to hold captives in war or inferior races as slaves.   "Before permanent Government exists," we are told, "and in many cases after it is considerably developed, the rights of each individual are asserted and maintained by himself, or by his family."   In such a condition one would think the rights of the individual, except so far as checked by the customs of his family and tribe, are pretty nearly commensurate to his strength and his cunning.

The following paragraph contains a very significant recognition of the function of war in the development of political societies : "Those ancient societies which progressed enough to leave records, having all been conquering societies," etc.[2]   But soon after this we have a statement about "the omnipresent control, which the Eastern nations in general exhibited"[3]—a curious view of Oriental history, where "anarchy *plus*

---

[1] *The Man versus the State*, p. 66.
[2] *Ibid.*, p. 93.   [3] *Ibid.*, p. 94.

the tax-gatherer" has been the general rule.   According to Maine [1] the Roman empire is the *first* instance of a *legislating* empire.   In the Persian "empire" everything was left to local customs, so long as taxes were paid to the great king; and this is the general type of Eastern rule.   This control, we are next told by Mr. Spencer, "was exhibited also in large measure by the Greek, and was carried to its greatest pitch in the most militant city, Sparta."   This remark is more accurate; but then the Greek cities belong to a very highly developed stage of political existence; and even with regard to them it is an exaggeration. Sparta appeared to Plato and Aristotle an *exception* among Greek cities in regulating the lives of its citizens.   "Similarly during mediæval days throughout Europe .   .   .   there were scarcely any bounds to governmental interference."   What has become of history?   Did not emperors and kings yield to priests, and bargain with their own feudal vassals? Did not the nobles of Aragon take a merely conditional oath of allegiance to their king: "We who are as good as you choose you for our king and lord, provided that you observe our laws and privileges; and if not, not"—a contract which Mr. Spencer

---

[1] *Early History of Institutions*, lecture xiii.

might plausibly, but erroneously, have quoted as an
argument for " natural rights " ?   " With the increase
of industrial activities . . .   there went . . . a
decrease of meddling with people's doings."   Well,
on this head I have said something already.   This
course of history, this transition from status to contract, Mr. Spencer appears to interpret as a struggle
in which the individual has gradually won his natural
rights from the State.   " Throughout a large range
of conduct the right of the citizen to uncontrolled
action has been made good against the pretensions of
the State to control him." [1]   Is not this an admission
that natural rights appear, not at the beginning, but
at the end of a long process ?   But if so, what was
the relevancy of Mr. Spencer's illustration of natural
rights from primitive races such as the Todas and
the peaceful Arafuras and all the rest of them ?   It
is becoming clear that, when people speak of natural
rights of liberty, property, etc., they really mean, not
rights which once existed, and have been lost, but
rights which they believe *ought* to exist, and which
would be produced by a condition of society and an
ordering of the State such as they think desirable.
There is an *eidolon* which leads men to put their

---

[1] *The Man versus the State*, p. 94.

golden age in the past, and to claim reforms under the guise of restoring ancient rights.

Fifthly, " reforms of law " are appealed to as proving that rights are not created, but recognised, by good laws.[1] That, of course, is the theory of the Roman jurists, the theory of "the law of nature which is the ground of all laws." Mr. Spencer is now in the company of the Stoics. How this is to be reconciled with the creed of evolution is not clear, unless Mr. Spencer will take a hint from Aristotle, and boldly admit that the true nature of a thing is to be found, not in its origin, but in its end: ἡ φύσις τέλος ἐστίν. But what then would become of his dictum that " we must interpret the more developed by the less developed "?[2] The only course is to recognise that the converse is also true ; and that besides going

---

[1] It is startling to find the Married Women's Property Act cited as an instance of the recognition of a natural right, unless a " natural right " equals " what ought to be." It is curious in what a series of abstractions the arguments about the political and social status of women are often carried on. The one side talk of woman's " sphere," as if that were something determinable *à priori:* they only mean " what . *is* been." The other side talk of " women's rights," as if they were something of which women had been deprived by the malice of men : they really mean those rights which they think *ought to be* conferred on women by a well-regulated society.

[2] *Data of Ethics,* p. 7.

to the Todas and the "peaceful Arafuras" to explain modern Governments, the reverse process must also be gone through. But this means a concession to a teleological view of the universe which we fear Mr. Spencer would regard as retrogressive. Mr. Spencer has a quite magnificent perception of half truths. What amazes the puzzled reader is how the halves do not oftener meet their other, and sometimes better, halves.

§ 6.   Does Society Grow, or is it Made?

In opposing government action Mr. Spencer does not always appeal to natural rights.   In the essay on "The Sins of Legislators" he has recourse to ideas which appear more congenial to his usual way of thinking.   Excessive legislation, he holds, arises from the prevalent ignorance of the organic structure of society, an ignorance which he ascribes to defects in the prevalent system of education.   The error prevails, "that society is a manufacture, whereas it is a growth"[1]: the conclusion apparently being, that Government ought to leave society alone, and let the struggle for existence go on ; and the result will be the survival of the fittest.   We may compare what is

---

[1] *The Man versus the State*, p. 74.

said in the essay on "The Coming Slavery" about
the law of nature, "that a creature not energetic
enough to maintain itself must die."[1] Government
interferes with that process of evolution which Mr.
Spencer would wish to contemplate with the calm
curiosity of an Epicurean god, but with a full, though
somewhat inexplicable, faith in the beneficent issue of
the long misery which the process causes to individual men, women, and children in the interest of the
species.   How this can be reconciled with his eager
defence of individual rights I fail to see, but shall
not inquire further.   At present I wish to ask how
it is compatible with his assertion that the remark of
Mackintosh, "*Constitutions* are not made, but grow,"
has become a truism.[2]   Nay, in this very paragraph
which I have now before me, I find "governmental
institutions" included in the "scientific conception of
society" as an organic structure.[3]   If Governments
"grow" very big and strong and fierce, why blame
them?   "For 'tis their nature to."   They cannot
help it, when they growl and fight and take to legislating in excess.   You need not blame the legislators

---

[1] *The Man versus the State*, p. 19.
[2] *Essay* on "The Social Organism," *init.*
[3] *The Man versus the State*, p. 74.

nor the constitution-makers, because on your own thesis they cannot *make* constitutions, however much they try. All is a growth. You might as well say to a man, " You must really make your head smaller; it is far too big for the rest of your body." I might reply to Mr. Spencer in the words which he himself quotes in *First Principles* (at the end of Part I.)—

> " Nature is made better by no mean,
> But nature makes that mean : over that art
> Which you say adds to nature, is an art
> That nature makes."

Here then is the dilemma : (1) If the Government is a part of the organic structure of society, and if the social organism is altogether an organism, and strictly grows, and cannot be made, Governments, like everything else, must, by necessity, be left to fight it out. The fittest will survive. If the Government is fittest, it will get the better of the individual (to assume for the moment Mr. Spencer's antithesis between them) ; if the individual is fittest, he will get the better of Government. Societies with much developed Governments must fight it out with societies with stunted Governments. The fittest will survive. Whatever is, is right ; and the legislator can have no sins, because he is only a part of the great movement which Mr. Spencer contemplates from those serene

heights of the system of synthetic philosophy which
are illumined by the beneficent radiance of the
Unknowable.   If any one thinks this accusation
of fatalism unwarranted, let him turn to p. 64 of
The Man versus the State : " As I heard remarked
by a distinguished professor, whose studies give ample
means of judging—'When once you begin to interfere with the order of Nature, there is no knowing
where the results will end.'   And if this is true
of that sub-human order of Nature to which he
referred, still more is it true of that order of Nature
existing in the social arrangements produced by
aggregated human beings."   The obvious conclusion
being, *Laissez faire*—with a vengeance.   But even
in these words notice how interference is spoken of,
as if Government was something outside the natural
structure.

(2) If, then, Government is outside the process of
evolution, how can we avoid the suspicion that there
is some flaw in Mr. Spencer's scientific conception of
society, and that it breaks down at Government ? So
that, after all, there was some need for Mackintosh to
say, " *Constitutions* are not made, but grow "; since
to Mr. Spencer the proposition does not appear
true.

A dilemma is apt to suffer from an incomplete

disjunction in the premisses. One suspects therefore that the choice does not lie solely between "making" and "growing," and that social organisms differ from other organisms in having the remarkable property of making themselves ; and the more developed they are, the more consciously do they make themselves.[1] But if so, an appeal to the fact that society is an organism is no argument either for or against government interference in any given case.

The truth is, that society (or the State) is not an organism, because we may compare it to a beast or a man ; but because it cannot be understood by the help of any lower—*i.e.* less complex—conceptions than that of organism. In it, as in an organism, every part is conditioned by the whole. In a mere aggregate, or heap, the units are prior to the whole ; in an organism the whole is prior to the parts—*i.e.* they can only be understood in reference to the whole. But because the conception of an organism is more adequate to society than the conception of an artificial compound, it does not follow that it is fully adequate. We have just seen that a one-sided

---

[1] Cp. Fouillée, *La Science Sociale Contemporaine,* p. 114 : "Plus un organisme est contractuel, plus il est vraiment organisé." On p. 115 he defines human society as " un organisme qui se réalise en se concevant et en se voulant lui-même."

application of the conception of organic growth leads to difficulties, as well as the conception of artificial making.   These we can only escape by recognising a truth which includes them both.   We must pass from "organism" to "consciousness," from Nature to the spirit of man.

The history of progress is the record of a gradual diminution of *waste*.   The lower the stage the greater is the waste involved in the attainment of any end. In the lower organisms nature is reckless in her expenditure of life.   The higher animals, more able to defend themselves, have the fewest young.   When we come to human beings in society, the State is the chief instrument by which waste is prevented.   The mere struggle for existence between individuals means waste unchecked.   The State, by its action, can in many cases consciously and deliberately diminish this fearful loss ; in many cases by freeing the individual from the necessity of a perpetual struggle for the mere conditions of life, it can set free individuality and so make culture possible.   An ideal State would be one in which there was no waste at all of the lives, and intellects, and souls of individual men and women.

II.

THE STATE *VERSUS* MR. HERBERT
SPENCER.

IN the foregoing essay I have endeavoured to point out the inconsistency between Mr. Spencer's political individualism and the scientific conception of society, which he himself has done so much to develop and to teach. The former is a "survival" from the so-called "philosophical radicalism," which flourished in Mr. Spencer's early days, and it is a survival which vitiates his whole political thinking. In the present essay I propose to examine a few other points in Mr. Spencer's attack upon the State.

§ I. THE SINS OF LEGISLATORS.

In the essay on "The Sins of Legislators," Mr. Spencer appears to maintain that, because governments in the past have made great errors, therefore they can never be trusted to do well ; [1] because sumptuary laws were mistaken, sanitary legislation is mischievous. Is there not such a thing as *learning by blunders* in individual life ? And may not a

---

[1] *The Man versus the State*, p. 48.

nation learn in the same way? Because we have
been unsuccessful hitherto in one direction, are we
to give up every attempt in other directions? "To
behave well, do nothing at all," thought Hans, the
awkward youth in the German story; and Mr. Spencer appears to think with him. I might as well
argue that because (in Mr. Spencer's opinion) all
philosophers in the past have been mistaken, therefore Mr. Spencer must be mistaken also. On the
other hand, he argues that, since inventions have
been made and trade has grown and languages have
been developed without the State doing anything,
government action should not be much esteemed.[1]
I might perhaps similarly argue that, because all
these good things have come about without Mr.
Spencer's philosophy, therefore Mr. Spencer's philosophy is of little worth; but I am aware that
such a mode of argument is fallacious, and think
it more important to raise the question, Whether
all these good things have happened without the
help of the State? Mr. Spencer's inductions,
derived presumably from the tables of descriptive sociology, remind one of the story (referred
to by Bacon) about the votive offerings hung up

---

[1] *The Man versus the State*, p. 63.

by those who escaped shipwreck, nothing being said about those who had been drowned. Mr. Spencer's historical scraps are like these votive offerings. The ill successes of English sanitary legislation are recounted, but nothing is said about those countries which have had no sanitary legislation at all (pp. 57, 58, and note on p. 57). It is true, that where there are no drains at all, there can be no typhoid fever produced by bad drains; in the good old days before sanitary legislation they had the plague instead. "Uninstructed legislators," we are told, "have continually increased human suffering in their endeavours to mitigate it." Of course we do not know what blessed results might follow from legislators brought up on Mr. Spencer's writings, or perhaps from hereditary legislators in whom the whole system of synthetic philosophy had by descent acquired the character of relatively *à priori* truth. We can only compare countries we actually know about; and though doubtless our uninstructed legislators have blundered frightfully, yet we think, on the whole, we are not so badly off as some people who have never had Parliaments to make blunders at all. Let us improve our legislature, educate our legislators, codify our laws, by all means; but it is childish to argue that, because three thousand Acts of Parlia-

ment have been repealed, it is a mistake to pass any.[1]
If your clothes do not fit you, that is no reason
for going naked. If the State had done nothing in
the past, we should be infinitely worse off, and *we
should not know so well the evils we have to remedy.*
It is nonsense to speak as if legislation in the past
had been one continued failure. Many of these Acts
of Parliament have been "repealed," not because
they are useless or mischievous, but because they
have proved so useful that new Acts have been passed
extending their principles and applications or con-
solidating previous legislation on the subject. In
any case, Mr. Spencer surely cannot deny the
advantages States have conferred on trade by coining
money, opening up roads, making harbours, providing
lighthouses, etc. If he questions this, let him only
consider the condition of trade in places where the

---

[1] *The Man versus the State*, p. 50. "As to the mistakes and
failures [of government]," says Lord Pembroke, in his pamphlet
on *Liberty and Socialism*, published by the Liberty and
Property Defence League, "what would private enterprise look
like if its mistakes and failures were collected and pilloried in
a similar manner? Law is nothing but public opinion organised and equipped with force, however grave the questions
affecting such organisation and equipment may be ; and so far
from law being always a worse thing than private action, the
difference between them is in many cases simply the difference
between civilisation and barbarism " (pp. 39, 40).

State, being in a rudimentary stage, has done nothing of the sort. Of course some people might argue that men were better off without trade ; but I do not think Mr. Spencer would take that line.

As to the education of legislators, it is interesting to find Mr. Spencer repeating the doctrine of Socrates. " Unquestionably among monstrous beliefs, one of the most monstrous is, that while for a simple handicraft, such as shoe-making, a long apprenticeship is needful, the sole thing which needs no apprenticeship is making a nation's laws " (*The Man versus the State*, p. 75).[1] Those who have wasted

---

[1] Mr. Auberon Herbert, who, if one may be allowed the expression, out-Herberts Mr. Herbert Spencer in his advocacy of *laissez faire*, demands that the politician, like the physician or the astronomer, should act upon general principles. (See *For Liberty*, pp. 14, 15.) Between the politician and the astronomer there is no analogy ; between the politician and the pilot there may be. And what should we think of a pilot (in the days before the mariner's compass) who made no allowance for local squalls or the varying depth of the water, or the force of currents, but looked only at the stars, because their movements follow definite laws which he has learnt from the astronomer? And what should we think of the physician, who, having got into his head some maxim about the *vis medicatrix naturæ*, used a treatment of *laissez faire* alike in cases of fevers and of fractures? If the physician's art were like the art of Mr. Herbert's statesman, it would no longer be " long "—neither would the lives of his patients.

their time on the Greeks have heard something like this before. But would a training such as Mr. Spencer would give the legislator-apprentice mend matters much? Mr. Spencer has not yet got beyond Socrates and Plato to find out with Aristotle that there is a difference between the ways in which natural science and politics have to be taught and learnt. We fear that the "systematic study of natural causation, as displayed among human beings socially aggregated" (p. 60), if Mr. Spencer's tables of descriptive sociology and his conclusions from them are a fair specimen, would not improve the stuff of which statesmen are made. Appropriate quotations from Horace will not make a statesman; but neither will misapplied metaphors from the laboratory. As an English statesman has to legislate for human beings and not for oysters, a study of the political problems of Athens and Rome will probably be at least as useful to him as an examination of the digestive processes of molluscs. We make a false antithesis between "classical" and "scientific" education. There is a more real antithesis between humanist studies and the sciences of Nature; a true national culture can dispense with neither of the two groups.

§ 2. NEGATIVE REGULATION.

"But, of course," Mr. Spencer might object to our criticisms " I do not wish government to do nothing. I wish it to act thoroughly in its proper sphere, which it will do all the better if it sticks to it. In the industrial stage of society on which we have now entered, government ought to be only negatively regulative. Government should redress evils which have happened, but ought not to interfere with natural rights and freedom of contract in order to prevent them happening." Mark, however, that Mr. Spencer would allow civil suits to be carried on at the expense of the State—*i.e.* of the community.[1] Thus, in Mr. Spencer's ideal State, I may

---

[1] *Political Institutions*, p. 748: " Those same changes which have cut off so many political functions at that time exercised, have greatly developed this essential and permanent political function. There has been a growing efficiency of the organisation for guarding life and property ; due to an increasing demand on the part of citizens that their safety shall be insured and an increasing readiness on the part of the State to respond. Evidently our own time, with its extended arrangements for administering justice, and its growing demand for codification of the law, exhibits a progress in this direction ; which will end only when the State undertakes to administer civil justice to the citizen free of cost, as it now undertakes, free of cost, to protect his person and punish criminal aggression on him."

have simultaneous suits going on against the speculative builder from whom I purchased my inse-
cure and insanitary dwelling; against the water
company that agrees to supply me with water, and
does supply me with diluted sewage; against the
milkman, who adulterates this same "water" with
chalk; against the butcher, who sends me diseased
horse-flesh as prime beef; against my doctor, who
of course requires no State-sanctioned diploma to
interfere with his individual enterprise, and whom I
suspect of having mangled one of my relatives;
against my free-trade druggist, who has nearly
poisoned myself; against my right-hand neighbour,
who feeds pigs in his garden; and my left-hand
neighbour, who keeps a liquor shop open day and
night, where he sells methylated spirits as good
whisky. Of course these lawsuits will cause me some
worry, since all these people will in turn prosecute
me for defamation of character, and they will waste
much time; but I shall have the practical satisfaction of knowing that they are all carried on at the
public expense—that is to say, at the expense of my
poorer fellow-citizens, who cannot afford to lose a
day's wages in attending the law courts to prosecute
the manufacturer, whose unfenced machinery has
devoured their daughters, and the ship-owner, whose

highly insured coffins have drowned their sons. And I shall have the theoretic satisfaction of admiring a *régime* of free contract, of individualism checked 'only by counter-individualism, and of studying in human beings the interesting problem of the survival of the fittest. But apart from practical inconvenience, here is a result puzzling to theory; what, according to our benighted views of politics, are offences against the State, will in Mr. Spencer's ideal epoch of individualism and industrialism be offences against the individual. Gradually all criminal offences will come to be regarded as civil offences (especially as the State is going to administer civil justice free of cost), and the primitive age will return when offences against the State were unknown. The whole course of legal " progress," as we have imagined it,[1] will be reversed. We shall thereupon relapse into the condition of the Todas and the peaceful Arafuras, who interest Mr. Spencer so much more than those foolish Greeks who invented the abomination of the State.

Mr. Spencer's ideal State—but perhaps I mistake. Mr. Spencer's ultimate ideal is one in which there is no longer any possibility of conflict, in which

---

[1] See Maine's *Ancient Law*, pp. 369, ff.

the individual has completely adapted himself to his environment—an ideal which will be realised when the individual is in his grave, and mankind and all living things have disappeared from a perishing planet. Life Mr. Spencer defines as adaptation of the individual to his environment ; but, unless the individual manages likewise to adapt his environment to himself, the definition would be more applicable to death.[1]

It must not be supposed that we wish to blind ourselves to the many real difficulties and objections which there are in the way of remedying and preventing evils by direct State action. If assured that the end is good, we must see that the means are sufficient and necessary, and we must be prepared to count the cost. But, admitting the real difficulties, we must not allow imaginary difficulties to block the way. In the first place, as already said (p. 10.), State action does not necessarily imply the direct action of the central government. Many things may be undertaken by local bodies which it would be unwise to put under the control of officials at a distance. "Municipalisation" is, in many cases, a much better "cry" than "Nationalisation." Ex-

---

[1] Cp. Sorley, *Ethics of Naturalism*, pp. 214, 215.

periments may also be more safely tried in small
than in large areas, and local bodies may profit by
each other's experience. Diffusion of power may
well be combined with concentration of information.
" Power," says J. S. Mill, [1] "may be localised, but
knowledge to be most useful must be centralised."
Secondly, there are many matters which can more
easily be taken in hand than others by the State
as at present constituted. Thus the means of com-
munication and locomotion can in every civilised
country be easily nationalised or municipalised,
where this has not been done already. With regard
to productive industries, there may appear greater
difficulty. But the process now going by which the
individual capitalist more and more gives place to
enormous jointstock enterprises, worked by salaried
managers, this tendency of capital to become "im-
personal," is making the transition to management
by government (central or local) very much more
simple, and very much more necessary, than in the
days of small industries, before the "industrial
revolution" began. The State will not so much
displace individual enterprise, as substitute for the
irresponsible company or "trust" the responsible

---

[1] *Representative Government,* chap. xv.

public corporation. Thirdly, and lastly, be it observed that the arguments used against "government" action, where the government is entirely or mainly in the hands of a ruling class or caste, exercising wisely or unwisely a paternal or "grandmotherly" authority—such arguments lose their force just in proportion as government becomes more and more genuinely the government of the people by the people themselves. The explicit recognition of popular sovereignty tends to abolish the antithesis between "the Man" and "the State." The State becomes, not "I" indeed, but "we." The main reason for desiring more State action is in order to give the individual a greater chance of developing all his activities in a healthy way. The State and the individual are not sides of an antithesis between which we must choose ; and it is possible, though, like all great things, difficult, for a democracy to construct a strong and vigorous State, and thereby to foster a strong and vigorous individuality, not selfish nor isolated, but finding its truest welfare in the welfare of the community. Mr. Spencer takes up the formula "from status to contract" as a complete philosophy of history. Is there not wanting a third and higher stage in which there shall be at once order and progress, cohesion and liberty, socialistic—but, *therefore*, rendering possible the highest development of all such individuality as constitutes an element in well-being? Perhaps then Radicalism is not turning back to an effete Toryism, but advancing to a further and positive form, leaving to the Tories and the old Whigs and to Mr. Spencer the worn-out and cast-off creed of its own immaturity.

§ 3. SOVEREIGNTY.

Mr. Spencer, in his case against the State, objects to its action, not only on the ground that the individual has a definite sphere within which it must not trespass, not only that State action has in the past been bad and adverse to progress, but that the State —he means the government—is always necessarily in a minority, and has no "divine right" to control individuals. He appears to have adopted from Hobbes and Austin the abstract conception of sovereignty, according to which sovereignty always resides in some definite person or persons, while he rejects their accompanying doctrine that sovereignty is unlimited.[1] Now in this he seems to me to have just chosen the false and rejected the true element in their political thinking. Sovereignty must be con-

---

[1] *The Man versus the State,* p. 78 ff.

ceived of as unlimited, else it is not sovereignty. A
limited sovereign is a sovereign that is not sovereign.[1]
In every independent political community there must
be some power which is ultimate, to which in the
last resort the appeal can be made.   If there were a
world-empire or a "federation of the world," there
would be in the last resort only one sovereign power,
the whole of mankind.   But, in so far as nations are
still relatively to one another in "a state of nature,"
in each nation there must be some power which is
supreme.   But this power can never reside in one
person or in any definite number of persons; and
this is the mistake alike of Hobbes and of Austin, a
mistake which has been exposed with such admirable
clearness by Sir Henry Maine, that it is only necessary to refer to the twelfth lecture of his *Early
History of Institutions.*[2]   Political obedience is never

---

[1] Of course it will be understood that I am using the word
in a technical sense, not in the sense in which we still call an
ornamental monarch a sovereign lord or lady, which is only a
survival in language.

[2] The only exception one might wish to take to what he there
says (p. 359), is that a method of abstraction which leads to
results to which no facts correspond is not *philosophically*
legitimate, however useful it may be as a provisional hypothesis
in science.   The business of the philosopher is to get beyond
the abstractions of ordinary thinking and of ordinary science.
In his *Popular Government*, Sir H. Maine seems to have fallen
away from his earlier opinion, and speaks (pp. 7 and 8) as if

habitually rendered to the uncontrolled will of a person or determinate number of persons but to this will
along with and controlled by " the whole enormous
aggregate of opinions, sentiments, beliefs, superstitions, and prejudices, of ideas of all kinds, hereditary
and acquired, some produced by institutions and
some by the constitution of human nature "—and all
this the analytical jurists leave out of account in their
theory of sovereignty.

There is a sense in which Austin's theory of
sovereignty may be made true, but it is not the sense

the sovereignty of the ruler and the sovereignty of the nation
were opposing theories which could be compared with and
measured against one another. But the former sovereignty is
a sovereignty of definite persons, the latter is indefinite. It is
quite true that, where human beings are divided into a ruling
and a subject *caste*, there we seem to get a definite division, but
among the ruling caste we have still to ask where sovereignty
resides, and, on Sir H. Maine's own showing, it cannot be
found among definite persons—unless in a State which is on
the eve of a revolution—but in the *opinions* of the community.
Democracy seems to have frightened him into abstractions
which he once combated.

Mr. F. Harrison, in the *Fortnightly Review* (vol. xxx., 1878),
denies that Austin's theory is either historical or philosophical :
it is only true for the lawyer. But this was not what Austin
meant. In the hands even of its apologists Austin's theory
becomes gradually less and less. We can make the propositions of Austin's jurisprudence, like some of the doctrines of
Ricardo's political economy, true by gradually divesting them
of application to reality.

in which Austin propounds the theory. The *legal* sovereign—*i.e.* the authority behind which the lawyer *quâ* lawyer will not and cannot go—must be definite.[1] In this sense the British Parliament is sovereign. It is omnipotent ; *i.e.* it can in theory do anything except what is physically impossible. In countries where a distinction is made between constituent and legislative assemblies, the sovereign is that body, whatever it may be, which can alter the constitution. But this legal sovereign is not the *political* sovereign, for which Austin professes to be looking. Behind the House of Commons is the electorate, as Austin himself recognises ; and behind the electorate is something vaguer but not less important—public opinion, the will of the people, the spirit of the nation itself.[2]

Rousseau's conception of the sovereignty of the people, the "general will," as distinct from the "will of all," contains a greater truth than the abstract conception of Hobbes and Austin. The Czar of all the Russias rules by the will of his people, as much as does the executive of the Swiss Federation. The belief in the Czar's divine right is the source of his power and the ground of their obedience. The

---

[1] See Professor Dicey's *Law of the Constitution*, p. 68 (Ed. 3).
[2] See Note B, "The Conception of Sovereignty."

difference between two such cases is that the general will has found a more adequate way of expressing itself in the one instance than in the other. The general will expresses itself by opinion in speaking and writing, as well as by electing representatives. When prevented from such means of utterance, it expresses itself by prostration before a God upon earth or by assassination, both of which are very inadequate ways. Rousseau's mistake consisted in his supposing that such a sovereign as "the people" can be formed by a contract between individuals, and that the general will of such a sovereign can only be expressed by an assembly of all the individuals who compose the people. He turns the general will into the will of all. He ignores the truth, which to abstract logic appears absurd, that an organic whole is not merely the sum of its parts. The body corporate is mysterious, if any one likes to call it so, mysterious like the personality of the individual. Emperors, kings, councils and parliaments, or any combinations of them are only the temporary representatives of something that is greater than they. "*Principes mortales, respublica æterna.*" This sovereignty of the people, this general will, is only an idea, it will be said. It is an idea; but not therefore unreal. It is real as the human spirit is real, because

it is this very spirit striving for objective manifes-
tation. It lives, and grows, and becomes conscious
of itself. It realises itself in different forms, in the
family, the clan, the city, the nation, perhaps some
day in the federation of the world.

§ 4. THE RIGHT OF MAJORITIES.

Since Mr. Spencer has adopted an abstract conception of sovereignty, it is no wonder that he is
puzzled over "the divine right' of majorities."[1] It is
obvious that the majority of a majority of a majority
may be arithmetically a very small minority of the
whole. Therefore, it is inferred, there is no reason
why a cabinet (*i.e.* its majority), which has the confidence of a House of Commons (*i.e.* of its majority),
which has the confidence of the nation (*i.e.* of its
majority), should have any particular authority to
dictate to us. Of course this way of arguing is only
valid if the nation is *merely* an aggregate of individuals, an idea which comes strangely from one who
talks about a social organism.

Mr. Spencer speaks of "an incorporated nation,"
and says that its members are bound "severally to
submit to the will of the majority *in all matters con-*

---

[1] *The Man versus the State*, p. 82.

cerning the fulfilment of the objects for which they are incorporated ; but in no others." [1]   But then Mr. Spencer apparently claims to decide for what objects we are an incorporated nation.   He claims to have drawn up the terms of agreement, to have drafted the deed of the original compact.   He is aware of the objections to the social contract theory, he gives rejoinders and "re-rejoinders," and finally concludes that the question to ask is : "What would be the agreement into which citizens would now enter with practical unanimity ?"   I do not see what "practical unanimity" means unless we fall back on a majority.   And I find that Mr. Spencer, when he polls the nation on the duty of resisting invasion, is going to leave out "the Quakers, who having done highly useful work in their time, are now dying out" [2]; and so this poor dying minority are going to have no rights in Mr. Spencer's State.   This does seem a very ancient and time-honoured way of treating the rights of minorities, and securing a "practical unanimity."   Again, when he polls the nation on the question of the protection of private property, he is going to omit the criminal classes—a large and influential section of the community.   Nay, further,

---

[1] *The Man versus the State,* p. 83.   [2] *Ibid.,* p. 85.

when he comes to deal with the land question, the votes of those who consider themselves landowners are apparently not to be counted. " Since the State is still supreme owner (every landowner being in law a tenant of the Crown), able to resume possession, or authorise compulsory purchase at a fair price, the implication is that the will of the majority is valid respecting the modes in which, and the conditions under which, parts of the surface or sub-surface may be utilised." Verily, if any of the distinguished members of the "Liberty and Property Defence League" have been drawing any consolation from having an anti-socialistic champion in the greatest living English philosopher, they will soon find this apologist of individualism a dangerous ally. Let Mr. Henry George convince "a majority" of Englishmen of his views about "the modes in which, and the conditions under which, parts of the surface or sub-surface may be utilised," and the Liberty and Property Defence League will fare no better than the Social Democratic Federation, the Quakers and the criminals. Mr. Spencer will secure "a practical unanimity" by omitting all their votes.

Other people would draw up the terms of agreement for the incorporated nation differently from Mr. Spencer, and some of us believe, with

Burke, that the State is not simply a joint-stock company or a private club. Some of us really do believe that, in some respects, society is an organism, though perhaps we do not repeat our creed so often as Mr. Spencer. As to the right of minorities, it may be enough at present to point out that the most important and valuable right of a minority is the right to turn itself into a majority if it can— *i.e.* the right of freedom of speech and freedom of association, not the impossible right of the member to exist apart from the organic whole. History shows us that a minority with intelligence, energy, and faith in their cause may hope with a fair chance for ultimate victory, if their cause is really the cause of humanity. One hundred men are numerically more than ten, and ten than one ; but the genius and earnestness and contagious enthusiasm of one and the strong coherence of ten will outweigh in the end the isolated apathy of many thousands. It is the very chief advantage of democracy over oligarchy that, while it establishes the power of the majority, it puts that majority potentially in the hands of those who have ideas and are able to make them spread. For the wise statesman of a free country is not the man who has a mere private theory of his own and imposes it on a passive and subject class, but the man who sympathetically comprehends the vague wants, the unformulated aspirations of the half-blind, half-dumb many whom he serves by leading. As a leader he is in advance of others, not because his ideas are not theirs, but just in so far as he can understand and express what they only feel.

A people who, like the Russian peasantry, accept only a unanimous decision as binding, have advanced a very small way in political development. The discovery that "counting heads would save the trouble of breaking them" marks one of the greatest advances that mankind have made in their hard upward course. The discovery of the "organic" system of representation marks another, and the significance of "public opinion" a still further stage. The acts of the government in every country which is not on the verge of a revolution are not the acts of a minority of individuals, but the acts of the un-crowned and invisible sovereign, the spirit of the nation itself.[1]

---

[1] A mere *plébiscite*, a mere *yes* or *no* of a bare majority, is a very bad, because "abstract" and "inorganic" way of arriving at the general will; on the other hand a *referendum, after* decision by representative bodies, may, in some cases, be a convenient manner of getting the "royal assent" or veto of the sovereign people.

§ 5. THE MEANING OF HISTORY.

Mr. Spencer's conception of the State helps us to understand his views on the subject of history. The antitheses of militant and industrial, *status* and contract, compulsory co-operation and voluntary co-operation, positively regulative and negatively regulative are certainly useful in their place; and I am very far from wishing to deny the services which have been done to the study of "human beings socially aggregated" by Mr. Spencer's sociological methods, although I do find that some other sociologists do not think very much of them.[1] But perhaps that is only the *odium sociologicum.* "Classical bias" and "Aryan prejudice," Mediævalism and Teutonism, and various other "isms," all tend to limit and distort our views of the past and the present; and it is useful to have characteristics from very different types of civilisation put side by side. Thus Mr. Spencer's story of the man who would not give the Maharajah Gulab Singh the customary rupee until his petition had been heard, is a most luciferous parallel to the procedure by which the English Commons secured their liberties

---

[1] See, *e.g.*, the Preface to Letourneau's *Sociology*, translation, p. viii.

by refusing to grant supplies till grievances had been redressed.[1] But there remains a great deal in human history, which cannot be fitted into one or another of the columns of a folio of " Descriptive Sociology." If we analyse the elements of a people's life and separate them off in this way, we are apt to miss just what is most significant about them. Again, the comparative and analytical methods which are applicable enough to people in a primitive stage of existence, who have no *history*, in the proper sense, fail when we come to peoples who have become conscious of their common life and of the significance of it. The ancient Hellenes or the modern English can hardly be treated in the same way as "the peaceful Arafuras."

In his very suggestive little book on *Education*,[2] Mr. Spencer says, " The only history that is of practical value is what may be called Descriptive Sociology." I fear that if the dreary folios, which a British public, capable of consuming five editions of *First Principles*, has yet been unable to swallow, are a fair sample of this descriptive sociology, this branch of science can never have a very practical

---

[1] *Political Institutions*, p. 433.
[2] Page 32 (cheap edition).

value in education. History with the human life
taken out of it, dead, dried, and sliced up into
columns, not even written in construable English,
might indeed be " crammed up " for an examination,
but with somewhat disastrous results on the intellect
of the patient. Mr. Spencer's contempt for the
personal element in history has been frequently
repeated,[1] but it is a contempt that is surely more
applicable to the school books of Mr. Spencer's in-
fancy, than to the history that is usually written now.
If the view which tends to split up history into a
series of biographies represents one extreme, surely
Mr. Spencer's reduction of history to a comparison
of scattered elements represents another, as fatal and
less interesting. If it is a mistake to think of the
history of the English Reformation as if it were
only the product of Henry VIII.'s change of wives,
an account of the Great Rebellion, which relegates
Charles I. and Oliver Cromwell to a thin column,
is equally mistaken and misleading. There are such
things as typical individuals, in whom great movements and great ideas, to which forgotten multitudes
have contributed, become embodied and realised,
and in whom alone they can be rightly understood.

---

[1] See, e.g., *Study of Sociology*, p. 58.

Mr. Spencer's mode of *historical judgment* is worth noticing. There is a remarkable passage in the *Study of Sociology*,[1] in which he contrasts the way in which the September massacres in the "Reign of Terror" and the campaigns of Napoleon are usually regarded, "Over ten thousand deaths we may fitly shudder and lament; two million deaths call for no shuddering and lamentation," etc., etc. I have no wish to exaggerate the horrors of the Red Terror —which are generally made most of by those who gloss over with a glib phrase the long agonies of White and Black Terrors, and who, expending their pathos on the sufferings of princes, have no tear of sympathy for the martyrdom of peoples—I have no wish to extenuate the cruelties of an ambition which made itself ridiculous by aping the follies and repeating the crimes of dynasties it had overthrown ; but we naturally and rightly distinguish between deaths inflicted in cold blood in the name of justice with a simulated form of trial and the inevitable and indiscriminate carnage of the battlefield. Crimes cannot be measured by the mere number of the victims.

What we mean by history and the value we put

upon it are questions of no small importance to us in this country and at this time. There is a fine passage at the end of M. Taine's little book called *A Study of John Stuart Mill.* The brilliant French writer describes his feelings on a summer morning in Christ Church Meadows, in Oxford. " Around, as though to guard them [the flowers in the meadows], enormous trees, four centuries old, extended in regular lines, and in them I found a new trace of that practical good sense which has accomplished revolutions without committing ravages; which, while reforming in all directions, has destroyed nothing ; which has preserved both its constitution and its trees ; which has lopped away dead branches without injuring the trunk ; and to which it is owing that this alone among the nations is in the enjoyment not only of the present but of the past." Let us, however, be sure that we are enjoying the past in the right way. There is a sentimental type of conservatism which preserves mischievous abuses because they are picturesque, and which supports those who preserve them because they are convenient to themselves ; but there is a true conservatism of national and social feeling with which the most thorough-going reformer can ill dispense. It is this which makes great changes possible and safe. It is, more-

over, a great mistake to leave the appeal to history
to the opponents of progress. History has shown
perpetually that it is impossible to stand still, and
that to do nothing is often to do the greatest wrong.
These seem truisms; but they are frequently forgotten. And they are forgotten most of all by those
who learn nothing from the past they profess to
reverence, who build the sepulchres of those whom
their fathers slew, and imitate their fathers' conduct
all the while. The heroes and the prophets belong
not to those who invoke their names, but to the
reformer who inherits their spirit by looking, as they
did, to the future. We may well turn again and
again to reflect on the noble works done for us by
our fathers in the old time before us, and we shall
best show our gratitude and requite our debt, not
by foolish maintenance of effete forms, but by endeavouring to do for others what they did for us;
that is to say, by endeavouring to hand on to those
that shall come after, the privileges we do *not* enjoy.

III.

INDIVIDUAL LIBERTY AND STATE INTERFERENCE.

§ 1. An Examination of J. S. Mill's "Liberty."

THE great interest of the political writings of John Stuart Mill lies partly in the fact that his thinking is in a process of transition from the extreme doctrines of individualism and *laissez faire*, in which he was brought up, to a more adequate conception of society. His candour makes his inconsistencies easily apparent; and the inconsistencies of a man of genius are always instructive. At present I wish to point out a few of the consequences which result from the abstract and mechanical or arithmetical way of regarding society as an aggregate of individuals, and of looking on government as a power whose influence is necessarily antagonistic to individual freedom.

I. Mill takes liberty in the merely negative sense of "being left to oneself." As he says (*Liberty*, chapter v.), "All restraint *quâ* restraint is an evil." Now if this only meant "Restraint *for which there is no reason* is an evil," that would be true enough. But *Ideally* in the context it means much more. The Pythago-

82

reans held that the unlimited was of the nature of evil, and limit of the nature of good. Mill inverts this. Yet, surely, it is only by restraint or limit that anything can be done. If you want to make a river useful, either for navigation or for turning mill-wheels, you must prevent it spreading itself at large over the fields ; you must hem it in a narrow channel, in order to give it regularity and force. If a man wants to do any good work in the world, he must restrict himself to certain things, and not go on dabbling vaguely in everything. To exalt liberty, in the sense of "absence of restraint," at the expense of restraint, is, as Sir James Fitzjames Stephen says, like praising the centrifugal force in the solar system and blaming the centripetal. Enthusiasm about a negation is enthusiasm thrown away. Sir. J. Fitzjames Stephen says much about liberty having this merely negative meaning. It has this meaning in Mill's book,[1] but in ordinary language it means very much more. The

---

[1] With a similar inclination for "the unlimited," Mill in his *Logic* (bk. ii., ch. vii., vol. i., p. 303, 8th edition) refers to such axioms as the "inconceivability of the opposite" as being, according to Mr. Spencer's view, "the *incurable limitations* of the human conceptive faculty" ; as if the capacity of thinking 2+2 =5, and such-like absurdities, would be an advantage to us. The *necessity* of mathematics, which Mill does not admit, is just their peculiar advantage.

liberty for which men have fought, and suffered, and died, is not the mere negative abstraction of "being left alone." [1] Political liberty means not mere absence of restraint, but freedom from arbitrary, illegal, unconstitutional, unwise restraint, and implies the positive side of subjection to good laws, which those who submit to them recognise as in some way made by themselves, whether directly, or through representatives, or by trusted rulers.[2] Liberty in its positive sense may therefore mean the sovereignty of law, as distinct from the sovereignty of individuals ; and if liberty comes to mean the absence of all law, we regard that as a corruption or degradation of liberty, and call it more properly "licence." Such merely negative "liberty" would practically mean the tyranny of the strongest.

---

[1] "*La loi et la liberté*" was the motto on a flag of the National Guard in the French Revolution.

[2] "Freedom is not what Sir Robert Filmer tells us : 'A liberty for every one to do what he lists, to live as he pleases, and not to be tied by any laws' ; but freedom of men under government is to have a standing rule to live by, common to every one of that society and made by the legislative power erected in it." Locke, *Treatise of Government* (book ii.), chap. iv., § 22. Cp. chap. vi., § 57 : "In all the states of created beings capable of laws, where there is no law there is no freedom. For liberty is to be free from restraint and violence from others, which cannot be where there is no law ; and is not, as we are told, 'a liberty for every man to do what he lists.'"

Mill gives an apparently more positive definition
of liberty when he says "Liberty consists in doing
what one desires." But this occurs to him only *à
propos* of a difficulty raised by the negative definition
of liberty. If you see a man stepping on to a bridge
which you know to be unsafe, you would feel justified in seizing him and holding him back. Now, if
liberty consists in being left to oneself, you were certainly interfering with his liberty. But, says Mill,
"Liberty consists in doing what one desires, and he
does not desire to fall into the river." This brings
us to the ambiguity in the word "desire." The man
desired to cross the bridge, and you interfere with
that particular desire, for the sake of furthering his
general desire to remain alive and dry. But on this
interpretation of liberty there is almost no limit to
the amount of interference or restraint which would
be justified. Thus a man desires to succeed in life,
but he engages in a business which you know will
not succeed. Then, according to Mill's view, you
would be justified in forbidding him to exercise the
trade he has chosen. The inquisitor torturing a
heretic might say, "This man desires salvation, and I
am seeking to prevent him being damned"; and of
course the inquisitor is as much convinced of the
unsoundness of the heretic's opinions, as you can be

of the unsoundness of some rotten planks. Thus we should arrive at an extreme opposite conclusion to that which Mill wishes to reach; and his defence of liberty would turn out to be an apology for despotism. It is the characteristic of an abstract theory to admit of quite opposite applications.

II. In the negative sense of absence of restraint liberty is obviously not an end but only a means; and, where there is a better result to be got by leaving alone, there that policy is to be chosen. In Mill's views about the supreme importance of individuality of character, we find, so far, the reason for the value he puts on the absence of restraint. Now, with regard to this, there are two questions to be asked: (1) Does Mill conceive of individuality aright? and (2) Will absence of restraint secure it?

1. Mill quotes Humboldt as saying: "The end of man is the highest and most harmonious development of his powers to a complete and consistent whole." [1] But when Mill explains what he means by individuality, we find that he takes it, like freedom, in the negative and abstract sense of diversity of one man from another; and he treats this diversity, this endless difference, as if it were a good thing in itself, an

---

[1] *Liberty*, chapter iii.

end to be pursued for its own sake. It is perfectly true that where there is no diversity, where all men are of one uniform type, every one doing exactly what his neighbours do, there we may be sure there is imperfect and stunted development. Goodness manifests itself in many ways. Genius is apt to appear eccentric. But Mill seems to convert the propositions, and to regard diversity and eccentricity as desirable in themselves. Originality is most precious, but as Sir J. F. Stephen says, "Originality consists in thinking for yourself, and not in thinking unlike other people."

2. It may very well be doubted whether absence of control would necessarily produce individuality, at least such individuality as constitutes "an element of well-being." As a matter of history, do we find that the growth of a settled State system and the elaboration of laws are adverse to the existence of individuality? A tribe of savages or barbarians are all very much more like one another in body and mind, than a similar number of civilised men of the same country. Among civilised men there is much greater variety of facial expression than among those at a lower stage. What certainly is true is, that in earlier times, when locomotion was more difficult in the world at large, or in any given country, there was a more picturesque

diversity. The inhabitants of one province or town differed more from that of another; but within each of these smaller areas it may be very much questioned whether there was as much scope for individuality as there is now. The man who differed from his neighbours too much ran a greater chance of exile or death than in times when the areas over which the same law prevails are larger. Undoubtedly in all transition from old to new institutions there is loss as well as gain. We cannot help that. The great thing is to endeavour that the gain shall always be much greater than the loss. There is an *Idolon* which we may call the "picturesqueness of the past." When we image to ourselves any past period which has proved worthy of being remembered with a personal affection,—that of itself limits us to a small portion of the whole human race, and to small periods of time,—we think at once of many places distant from one another, and yet we think only of a small number of persons, of the few who have been so conspicuous as to become historical characters. We forget the immense number of stupid, uninteresting, commonplace "Philistines," who must have been the contemporaries of Pericles, or of Dante; and we forget the great part of the lives of even the conspicuous people, which must have been commonplace, and "just like the lives of anybody else."[1] Again, the impression we sometimes get, that as time goes on individuality tends to disappear, is, to a great extent, due to the recognition that on the whole, as we come nearer our own times, the people we hear of are like ourselves, and therefore the feeling of strangeness dies away. But it is to a great extent want of imagination that makes people feel the life in which they are actually living deficient in interest. One of the main functions of art is just to teach us to see the world in which we live as we never saw it before, to recall the golden and heroic ages by opening our eyes to see them in the life we have despised as commonplace. The greatness of many a man is not recognised till he is dead;

---

[1] Cp. Machiavelli, *Discourses on Livy* (trans. by N. H. Thomson), book ii., preface : " Men do always, but not always with reason, commend the past and condemn the present, and are so much the partisans of what has been, as not merely to cry up those times which are known to them only from the records left by historians, but also, when they grow old, to extol the days in which they remember their youth to have been spent. And although this preference of theirs be in most instances a mistaken one, I can see that there are many causes to account for it, chief of which I take to be that in respect of things long gone by we perceive not the whole truth, those circumstances that would detract from the credit of the past being for the most part hidden from us, while all that gives it lustre is magnified and embellished."

for then only can people pick out what is really significant about him.

The average individual, if left to himself, is more likely to grow up just like his neighbours. The undisciplined character is more likely to be weak; and the individuality which is worth having should be based not on weakness but on strength. But this consideration suggests an important distinction. We must distinguish between the influence of Society and Custom over the individual, and the influence of the State and Law.

III. It is true that the State is society organised, and that law is custom regulated. But it does not follow that they will always act in the same direction —that law will always affect the individual in the same way that custom and opinion do, only with stronger force. To think this is to become a victim to that vice of abstraction against which we have constantly to be on our guard. Mill argues, in chapter iv. of his *Liberty*, as if society regulated and society unregulated, as if law and opinion always acted in the same direction, differing only in respect of the greater force belonging to the former. Now so far is this from being the case, that very often it is law (or the State) alone which can protect the individual against the excessive force of opinion and

the tyranny of custom. Many people may think a
man a scoundrel, but a well-regulated State protects
him against lynching and against libel. In what
we call "society" there are many associations or
communities besides the great community which we
call the State. There is the family (both in the sense
of *familia* or household, and in the sense of *gens* or
clan) ; there are all the various professions and trades,
whether explicitly organised in guilds and unions or
not ; there are all Churches and religious bodies ;
there are ancient and powerful corporations, with
charters and privileges and customary rights ; there
are also modern and powerful joint-stock companies ;
and there are all the various combinations between
man and man formed by contracts of all sorts. The
head of the household, if left to himself to act " like
the Cyclops" in patriarchal manner, might exercise
his *patria potestas* in a way which would interfere
with the just liberty—*i.e.* what we have come, or are
coming, to regard as the just liberty—of wife, children,
and servants. The State steps in to protect them by
direct legislation, or by sanctioning legal remedies
against the exercise of customary privileges with
which in the good old days it would never have
dared to meddle, or dreamt of meddling. The trades
guilds exercised an authority over individuals to

which the State has gradually put an end. The State has restrained religious bodies from exercising the control they wished over the opinions and conduct of individuals. We are beginning to find out that the powers of gas and water companies, and the relations between landlord and tenant, between employer and employed, nay, even between parent and child, frequently need State interference *in the interest of individual freedom.* Yet all these various subordinate associations of men contribute their share to the formation of that vague totality which we call "public opinion."

If we consider this difference between State control and the control of society or opinion, we can understand what would otherwise be inexplicable ; in a country where the State meddles less with the individual, society may meddle more, and *vice versâ.* Mill, with his usual candour, recognises this. " In England," he says, "the yoke of opinion is perhaps heavier, that of law lighter, than in most other countries of Europe." [1] But the full significance of this Mill fails to see. Most rightly and most necessarily he protests against that petty social tyranny which leads to so much hypocrisy, and which dwarfs

---

[1] *Liberty,* chapter i.

men and women, both intellectually and morally. The evil of such a tyranny of opinion is, however, no necessary argument against State control. On the contrary, it is sometimes only by a more effective State action that the individual can be saved from excessive social pressure. It is well to fight opinion with its own weapons ; but stronger arms are sometimes needed. Thus the State, in taking education from the hands of ecclesiastical bodies, or of close corporations, or at least by controlling such sects and corporations, interferes *in behalf of individual liberty.*[1]

IV. The word "interference" is dyslogistic ; it has an ugly sound, for nobody likes to be interfered with. The constant use of the term in discussions about the

---

[1] Mr. Spencer (*The Man versus the State*, pp. 111, 112) rightly protests against "filibustering" in the colonies. But is there likely to be more "filibustering" where there is a strong government, or where there is none at all ? I have not touched on the vexed question of intervention in foreign affairs. I would only point out that the usual discussions on the subject swarm with abstractions. Non-intervention cannot be a policy ; for it is an impossibility alike in internal and external affairs. Even where no other civilised nation is likely to pounce on a barbarous island, we do not escape responsibility if our traders destroy the population by "free trade" in rum, or carry them off as forced labourers by a mockery of "free contract." Not non-intervention, but *intervention only in the interests of humanity*, ought to be the watchword of those who dislike the spirit of aggression.

functions of government implies the false theory, that all that the State gains the individual loses. But, as we have just seen, State interference may mean individual protection ; the State may interfere in order to prevent some lesser body interfering. Compulsory education may be regarded as interference with the liberty of the parents, but it is interference in behalf of the liberty of the child. Interference with the freedom of bequest may be prevention of the tyranny of the " dead hand." Interference with freedom of contract may be protection of those who cannot protect themselves. That we can call a measure "interference" is no proof that the measure is bad ; we may be interfering with what is bad. It is no proof even that individual liberty—even in its quite negative sense—is being diminished.

V. If then State interference be not necessarily in itself a bad thing, nor necessarily hostile to liberty, when ought the State to interfere, and when not ? Mill lays down the rule that " the sole end for which mankind are warranted, individually or collectively, in interfering with the liberty of action of any of their number, is self-protection." [1] The State or society, he holds, can never rightly interfere with "that part

---

[1] *Liberty*, chapter i.

of a person's conduct which merely concerns himself."
He holds, on the one hand, that only protection of
other individuals can ever justify State interference
(though it may not always do so), and, on the other
hand, that acts which are merely self-regarding can
never rightly be interfered with by others. The conception of the individual appears here in its most
abstract and negative form. Mill disclaims a theory
of abstract rights, and yet his way of reasoning
implies it. He assumes the right of a person to
regulate for himself a definite part of his life independently of, and prior to, his existence as the
member of a community. It is clear that the
individual of whom Mill is *really* thinking is the full-
grown man who is capable of being influenced in his
conduct by the result of discussion—*i.e.* is capable of
guiding all his life by rational considerations—*i.e.* is a
person very like Mill himself. The individual in this
very fully developed sense is the product of a very
advanced civilisation, and is rare even in the most
advanced societies. Mill says, "Liberty as a principle
has no application to any state of things anterior
to the time when mankind have become capable of
being improved by free and equal discussion." If
we take this strictly, it limits the concession of liberty
much more than most people would care or would

dare to limit it. But this conception of the full-grown individual is taken apart from the only surroundings which make him possible; he is thus made into an abstraction; his only relation to others is that of difference and exclusion; his "self" and his "sphere" stand over against their "selves" and their "spheres." The real civilised individual, however, is no such mere negation; his true self he finds not in distinction and separation from others, but in community with them. We may very well doubt whether any acts, nay, even any thoughts, of the individual can, in the strictest sense, be merely self-regarding, and so matter of indifference to other individuals.[1] If we have our own best interests at heart, it is of the very greatest importance to us that all the people we have to do with should think as soundly and act as rightly as possible. We cannot separate our own interests in an abstract way from the interests of others, nor theirs from ours. The more we learn of nature, and the more we learn of human society, the more we discover that there are

---

[1] The Earl of Pembroke, in his pamphlet on *Liberty and Socialism* (published by the "Liberty and Property Defence League"), pp. 82, 83, admits that "hardly any actions are purely self-regarding." We ought to be very grateful to Lord Pembroke for his clear exposure of the principles on which his "League" rests.

S. I.   H

no absolute divisions, but that every atom influences and is influenced by every other. It may be very inexpedient to meddle with particular acts, or it may be practically impossible to do so ; but we can lay down no hard and fast line separating self-regarding acts from acts which affect others. We may use the distinction, as we use many others, with sufficient convenience in ordinary talk, but we must not suppose that it contains any magic light to guide us in life or in legislation.

§ 2. WHAT IS THE END OF THE STATE?

Neither the supposition of a definite sphere within which an individual's actions are merely self-regarding (a supposition which Mill expressly avows, and Mr. Spencer,[1] in spite of his biology, apparently implies), nor the old doctrine of natural rights (which Mr. Spencer expressly avows, and Mill, in spite of his Benthamism, apparently implies), nor Mr. Spencer's own special new theory of the social organism affords us any help in answering the question whether in any particular case government action is desirable or not.[2] Of course I do not intend to deny that each

---

[1] See Essay I.

[2] Cp. Lord Pembroke's pamphlet (referred to on last page), pp. 8, 56, 87. "We must make up our minds to give up the idea of discovering any single principle that will enable us in

of these conceptions has an intelligible meaning, if not abstractly interpreted, nor that they each and all have a value alike in historical explanation, and in practical discussion. There *is* a sphere of individual action into which we have come, or are coming, to see that other individuals ought not in a well-regulated society to intrude; this sphere is not, however, something fixed and known beforehand, but an ideal differing at different times, always more or less vague, and to be permanently secured only by the help of a strong, and vigorous, and enlightened State. There *are* natural rights; but these are not behind, but in front of political progress. Man is still struggling to know, as well as to attain, his true *nature*

all cases to set the proper boundaries to State action and protect the province of individual freedom." From this sentence, however, it is clear, that while Lord Pembroke admits the principle I contend for, he never gets rid of the mechanical way of regarding State action as if it were necessarily antagonistic to individual liberty, and a balance had to be struck, a compromise made between the two. "There must be some sort of compromise or compact existing between the individual and the society, and that compact must contain the principle, if such a principle there be. But if we inquire what the terms of this silent treaty are in the various races of the world, in the several stages of their development, we find that they are never the same" (p. 57). Did Locke leave the Social Contract theory as an heirloom in Lord Pembroke's family? It ought to be put in the British Museum.

and his just *rights.* The conception of organic
growth, if properly grasped, clears away mischievous
abstractions in politics and in history ; but politics
and history are not thereby turned into branches of
imaginative biology. In understanding human nature
and human society, we must have recourse to a set
of ideas which find hardly any place at a lower stage.
We have come into a realm of ends or aims, consciously sought. Problems of practical politics may
be discussed more profitably on the basis of the Utilitarianism of Bentham or Mill, than on the basis of
Mr. Spencer's incongruous mixture of "Natural
Rights" and physiological metaphor.[1]

It is often repeated that in ancient society the
individual existed for the sake of the State, but that
in modern society the State exists for the sake of the
individual. This is one of those antithetical common-
places whose partial truth is apt to be misleading.
One may safely take the Hellenic State as typical
of the ancient State, and Athens and Sparta as
the typical Hellenic States. The Athenian citizen
existed for Athens, it is true ; but did not Athens
exist for the Athenian citizen ? Any one who
doubts this may read again what Pericles—whom

[1] See Note C. "On Utilitarianism."

Mill takes as a type of well-developed individuality
—says in the "Funeral Speech," which Thucydides,
with at least dramatic truth, puts into his mouth.
The Athenian citizen should be ready to die for
Athens, because Athens offers so glorious a life of
freedom to the Athenian citizen. "But," it will be
said, "Sparta was very different." True, Sparta
could not have produced a Pericles. But the philosophers Plato and Aristotle, who to modern eyes
appear to exaggerate the functions of the State,
praise Sparta just because the Spartan constitution
was almost the only one which professedly aimed at
making its citizens good. The Spartan conception
of "goodness" was a very narrow one; but it was
the goodness of the individual citizens which was the
object aimed at, however unsuccessfully, by the life-
long restraint in which they lived. The ancient
State expected its citizens to live for it, and to die
for it, because it existed for them. It existed indeed
for them alone and not for the unenfranchised multitudes who were mere means to the State's existence,
and no part of the State itself. The Greek State
existed for the few: the modern State professes to
exist for all—and may do so some day in reality.
This is the true antithesis between ancient and
modern politics, which is falsely put, when it is said

that State and individual have changed places as end
and means. If we turn to the modern world, is it
true that the State is a mere means to individual
convenience? Is it not just those very men to
whom liberty has been a religion that have been most
ready to sacrifice ease, friendship, happiness, life itself, for what they conceived to be the good of their
nation? The popular and poetic instinct which has
united, as objects of devotion, freedom and father-
land, has more of truth in it than the arguments of
theorists, who see only individualism in liberty, and
in the requirements of the State always an evil, which
may sometimes be necessary.

The State has, as its end, the realisation of the
best life by the individual. This best life can only
be realised in an organised society—*i.e.*, in the State;
so that the State is not a mere means to individual
welfare as an end; in a way, the State is an end to
itself. Modern ethics would indeed generally add
that this best life of the individual cannot be completely realised in his particular nation, but only in
and along with the best life of humanity. Whether
there is an end for the individual outside of the end
for humanity is a question which some would raise.
In answer I shall only call attention to the fact,
that all healthy moralities and all healthy religions

(*i.e.*, all those which, if widely spread, would be compatible with the continued and flourishing existence of human society in this world) have placed the best life for man here in some sort of community with other men, and have conceived of any better life hereafter as still a life in community. The individual who cannot realise the possibilities of his spiritual nature in his earthly dwelling-place yet feels himself a citizen of the heavenly city, a member of the company of the elect of God.

But what is this best life? We cannot define it, we cannot formulate it, in any one word or phrase. It will be differently conceived of according to the measure in which it is realised. The ideal determines the actual, but is also determined by it. As humanity advances, as man comes to understand himself and his aims more and more, these aims appear to him in new forms. They change as he changes. Each generation has its own ideal of what is best and highest; and what proves itself to be best and highest in any generation may be taken as the measure and determination of that generation's ideal. The good man of any age is the standard of goodness in that age.

It may be objected to this brief account of the relation of State and individual in respect of their ends, that it involves the fallacy of arguing in a circle. "The State cannot be both end and means; the ideal cannot be produced by the age for which it is an ideal. Logic is against you." Well, then, let me answer boldly : So much the worse for logic ; *i.e.*, the abstract logic of mathematics or of mechanics is not applicable to what is organic or more than organic.[1] Wherever there is growth, there we must expect to find what will not fit into one or other of the alternatives of an antithesis. No one has solved the puzzle whether the hen or the egg comes first. We cannot understand the one without implying the

---

[1] As a fine specimen of Mr. Spencer's logic, may be taken this sentence from *Political Institutions*, p. 730 : "It is not so much that a social life passed in peaceful occupation is positively moralising, as that a social life passed in war is positively demoralising. Sacrifice of others to self is in the one incidental only, while in the other it is necessary. Such aggressive egoism as accompanies the industrial life is extrinsic ; whereas the aggressive egoism of the militant life is intrinsic." It is doubtless important to be informed that A is not not-A, but it becomes wearisome after a time, and we long to learn that A is B —*i.e.*, something other than merely itself. It is useful to know that a square is not a circle ; but it is more useful to know, even approximately, what square *is* any given circle. Even in mathematics, the logic of mere identity does not carry us far. "Industrialism," as we know it in the actual world, is not so separate from "militancy" as Mr. Spencer's distinctions would make us believe. Of course it would be possible to define each of them so as absolutely to exclude the other ; but the things thus defined would be ideas of Mr. Spencer's, and not realities.

other; and so it is with the individual and the State, with the actual morality of an age, and the ideal or end which determines that morality.

In the early forms of society, the conception of human well-being is limited to the well-being of the family or tribe to which the individual belongs. Morality for him is determined by the needs of his family or tribe. That is right which tends to its preservation, its being, and its *well*-being (for even in the earliest stage something more than mere continued existence enters, however dimly, into the conception of the social end). That is wrong which tends to decay or dissolution. The individual by himself has no morality ; but in the struggle for the welfare of the family we have already, in an elementary form, many of the virtues. As other communities grow up wider than the family, in answer to wants which it alone cannot meet, the ideal of excellence is changed. When we come to the highly developed city-state of the "classical" world, the civic virtues become the most prominent, sometimes threatening to crush out those of the family altogether. With the Roman Empire and the spread of Christianity there grew up the idea of a community of mankind, at least within the limits of the Roman world and of Christendom. The incursions of the northern barbarians restored their importance to the family and tribal virtues, but the decay of the empire and the prevailing type of religion caused the civic virtues to fall into comparative neglect. The rise of the modern nation has again given them a place in our more complex ideal. But beyond the nation there is growing up more and more the conception of the oneness of humanity—not now a mere speculative phrase, as with the Stoics, nor limited to one creed, as in the Middle Ages, but a definite element in our ideal however little it may as yet have modified political practice. The interests of humanity seem often to conflict with the interests of the nation, as the interests of the nation with those of the family. The child must learn in the little world of home or school the lessons to be used in the larger world outside ; and yet the virtues of manhood, needed in the larger world, are not exactly the same as those of childhood and youth. So it is in the " education of the human race." At each step in advance correction and modification are required. At each step, however, the duties and virtues of the individual are determined by the conception of a common good ; but this conception of common good. changes and grows with the progress of mankind. The very fact of progress makes abstract ethical precepts of little

value. They have only a general validity, and may
not fit the case where we wish to apply them. Our
ethical judgments are judgments about particulars,
and the same is true of our political judgments.
When any measure of State action is proposed, there
is little advantage to be got by asking whether this
is the sphere of the State? or whether it is meddling
with the sphere of the individual? as if every one
could tell, beforehand, without any particular experience, what these spheres were. They are what we
think they ought to be ; and they are not necessarily
mutually exclusive. It is much better to ask the
Utilitarian question : " Is this particular measure expedient in this case? " Bentham would ask, " Will it
tend to the greatest happiness of the greatest number ?"—a question profitless in its apparent precision.
We must alter it into the vaguer but less misleading
one: "Will it tend to the greater well-being, physical,
intellectual, moral, of mankind, or at least of that
portion of mankind which we can practically take
into account?" or we may put it : " Will it make
society healthier?"—a formula Mr. Spencer would
probably accept. For Mr. Spencer has admirably
used the Aristotelian analogy of health in explaining
morality. Healthy activities are (on the whole, and
in the long run) pleasant activities, and so the mis-

take has arisen of treating the accompanying pleasure, which is merely a conspicuous external trait, as
if it were the end to be sought. The doctrine of
Natural Selection, applied to society, has given a new
force and a new meaning to the Utilitarian theory,
while correcting its errors and its narrowness. If we
can foresee what will tend towards the common
welfare and adopt it, we shall save our society from
going to ruin by external attack or internal dissolution. The theory of Evolution, rightly understood,
gives no sanction to an *à priori* dogma of *laissez
faire.*

§ 3. How to Apply our Principles.

Our question about any particular measure, " Is it
for the good of those for whom we are legislating?"
might quite well be adopted by holders of opposite
views about the State. Some would reject a measure
because they think it better the individual should in
this case be left alone ; others would adopt it because they think in this case the individual needs
State protection. But, even before it is applied to
any particular case, the general question admits of
being divided into three special questions, which, following the guidance of Sir. J. Fitzjames Stephen,[1] we
may formulate thus :—

---

[1] *Liberty, Equality, Fraternity*, p 54 (Ed. 2.) : "Compulsion

1. Is the object aimed at good? (*i.e.*, as we have explained, will it tend to advance the well-being of the community?)

2. Will the proposed means attain it?

3. Will they attain it at too great an expense or not? (*i.e.*, can the end be attained without doing more harm than is compensated by the benefit of its attainment?)

If, now, we ask whether the Liberal—or what Mr. Spencer scientifically designates "the sub-species Radical"—is inconsistent in maintaining freedom of opinion and freedom of trade, while at the same time maintaining the expediency of compulsory education and of Factory Acts, both of which are interferences with complete freedom in money-making, and the former of which is capable of being represented as an interference with freedom of opinion also—if any abstract principle of individual *versus* government is to decide, the answer clearly is, as Mr. Spencer thinks, that he is inconsistent, and there is really a reaction in favour of Toryism.[1] But let me,

---

is bad (i.) when the object aimed at is bad; (ii.) when the object aimed at is good, but the compulsion employed is not calculated to obtain it; (iii.) when the object aimed at is good, and the compulsion employed is calculated to obtain it, but at too great an expense."

[1] *The Man versus the State*, pp. 1 ff.

leaving abstractions, put the question in its triple form, and see what results.

I. Let me take first the case of State regulation of opinion. Now it might be very desirable that all men should at all times think correctly, but this no State can secure. The State, however, *can* interfere with the utterance of opinion in conversations, speeches, and writings, because these are overt acts. Suppose we admit that it is desirable to regulate private conversation so that nothing immoral or irreligious (from any given point of view) should be uttered without punishment—*i.e.*, suppose we admit the end to be good. There still remains the difficulty, that we cannot attain this end without establishing a spy-system, which might be worse for the cohesion and welfare of society than the occasional hearing of some shocking remark. With public speeches and published writings the case is obviously different. It is of their very essence that they are public acts ; so that the State can more easily interfere, although the end of suppressing any particular opinion may not thereby be attained. Suppose we agree with the Russian Government that it would be highly desirable to exclude the works of Mr. Herbert Spencer from public libraries, and prevent them being publicly sold, we know quite well that that would only lead to their being devoured more eagerly in private, and with all the additional zest which, since the days of Eden, has accompanied the eating of forbidden fruit. If people have to smuggle their liquor or their literature, they will take care that they get it strong. The mischief of wrong opinions is thus intensified. Besides which, to check the free utterance of opinion may be to close a safety valve. Of course there are many distinctions which must be made. It may be expedient to leave untouched an opinion expressed in a book, especially if it is a large, or a scientific, or a dull book ; while the same opinion, expressed in a thrilling speech at an enthusiastic meeting, may be treated as an incitement to crime, or certain to promote a breach of the peace. A wise administration requires great tact and foresight in knowing when it can safely interfere. There is no *à priori* rule applicable alike in every case.

I have been arguing on the assumption that the end, viz., uniformity of opinion, is in itself desirable. There still remains the question :—Is uniformity of opinion on religious and moral matters a desirable thing for the welfare of any given community ? "Certainly," it may be said, "if they are *right* opinions." But how do we know that our opinions are right? Of course every one is convinced he is right; but if he really is, he should claim the power of convincing other people by other means than those of force. Uniformity of opinion, if obtained by force, may be only the crystallisation of error; and even if the opinion were right, but not really accepted, the result would be hypocrisy and intellectual and moral deadness. Only those who in cowardice or indolence have given up the irksome duty of thinking will allow their opinions to be dictated to them. This is the first argument against religious persecution—that the end proposed, uniformity of opinion, is a bad, or at least a doubtful end. But as I have already indicated, even if the end were undoubtedly a good one, there remain the further questions: (2) Will the means proposed attain it? and (3) at a cost we are prepared to meet? Now, one of the defects of a great many religious persecutions has been that the means adopted have not been sufficient to attain the end. Thus, the very occasional persecutions under the Roman Empire were not sufficient to repress Christianity, but only helped to give it greater coherence and vitality. On the other hand, if the compulsion is made as effectual as was the persecution of Protestantism in Spain, this can only be done at an enormous cost; powers which may become dangerous and inconvenient have to be given to certain bodies or persons, the country loses all those who will emigrate rather than surrender their beliefs, privacy is disagreeably interfered with, ordinary business is seriously deranged, feeling is embittered, and there is the risk of a successful or, at least, a troublesome revolt.[1] Thus, religious persecution is to be condemned, not because it is interference of the State (or of society) with what is merely self-regarding, nor because it is interference for other purposes than to protect individuals against other individuals. The religious zealot would deny both propositions ; he might say that a heretic was a greater danger to society than a man sick of the plague. Religious persecution is to be condemned, because it is an awkward means of obtaining what is possibly a doubtful end, and a means which cannot be used except at too great a cost. Persecution *quâ* persecution, like restraint generally, is neither good nor bad. Persecution is the name given to compulsion by the person who is compelled : and "compulsion" may or may not be a "blessed word"

---

[1] Cp. Locke's famous sentence : " Neighbourhood joins some and religion others. But there is one thing only which gathers people together into seditious communions, and that is oppression."

according to circumstances. The anti-vaccinators, who are fined for refusing to have their children vaccinated, or the " Peculiar People," who go to prison rather than interfere with Providence by getting medical advice for their dying little ones, complain that they are victims of persecution. The State answer to the latter would be : " You may think what you like about Providence ; but we know that the difference between medical treatment and its absence may mean the difference between life and death"; to the former, " You may use all freedom in making public your *opinion* about the inefficacy or the risk of vaccination ; but, in the meantime, we are acting according to the opinion of experts and the experience derived from hospital statistics, and therefore you must submit." Now the difference between such cases and religious persecution is this : There are available statistics about the relation between vaccination and immunity from small-pox, and, if necessary, better statistics can be procured ; but theological experts can produce no similarly trustworthy statistics—statistics of a kind that should satisfy a parliamentary commission—about the relation between orthodoxy (of any given species) and immunity from damnation. Therefore the State does well if it acts on the wise principle laid down, but, unfortunately, not always followed by Tiberius : *Deorum injuriæ dis curæ*—Wrongs against God are God's affairs. Or let both State and society listen to Gamaliel : "Refrain from these men, and let them alone : for if this counsel or this work be of men, it will be overthrown ; but if it is of God, ye will not be able to overthrow them ; lest haply ye be found even to be fighting against God,"—or let them listen to a greater than Gamaliel, who said, "Forbid him not, though he followeth not with us."

When some religious *observance* leads to a crime or to a breach of the peace, then the State may and does interfere ; but in such cases it is the wrong action that should be punished and not the *opinion* that is connected with it. In the same way, if blasphemy be punished at all (which seems to be highly inexpedient), it should be punished as an offence against other people and not as an offence against God. The belief that offences against God must be punished by human authority is the great source of that sin against humanity which we call religious persecution. This belief has to be rooted out of men's minds in order to secure religious freedom. It is impossible to maintain the abstract principle, "All persecution is bad" ; because we do not know what 'persecution" may be made to mean.

II. Let me turn now to Compulsory Education. That all should have at least a minimum of education to give them a fair chance of real freedom,—*i.e.*, of growing up intelligent, useful citizens,—we regard as so important an end, that we are prepared to cause a little friction, and to sacrifice a little money in order to obtain it. We insist on the child's chances in life being protected to some extent against the selfishness, ignorance, or superstition of parents. We desire the end, and we have counted the cost. Mr. Spencer would say, "This *protection* involves *aggression*."[1] Of course it does : it would be of no use if it did not. But we consider the protection in this case makes it worth while to aggress. We have no abstract prejudice against everything which anybody may call aggression. No doubt a burglar would regard the policeman, whom Mr. Spencer retains to exercise the "negatively regulative" functions of government, as an abominable aggressor on the liberty of the good old days.[2]

---

[1] *The Man versus the State*, p. 72.

[2] I have not touched on the further question of *free* education, as I wished to take my illustrations from the cases which are least disputed. Near the end of his *Political Institutions* (p. 746) Mr. Spencer seems to argue that the egoistic impulse will induce the citizen to resist paying for the education of other people's children, and the altruistic impulse will induce other

"But in bringing up children in State schools, are you not moulding their opinions in a particular groove, and is not that interfering with freedom of opinion?" If the State were minutely to direct and control the education of the universities, or even of the secondary schools, there might be some reason for asking this question. But is Mr. Spencer really afraid of a theological bias being imparted by means of the multiplication table, of a metaphysical system being introduced into the A, B, C, and of a Tory twist in the formation of pot-hooks? The freedom of opinion of those who cannot read and write, and will not let their children learn, does not seem to be a very precious thing. Those who have no tradition in favour of education are the least likely to appreciate its benefits, and the least competent to decide how they shall bring up their children. The existence of a mass of ignorance at the base of society is a grave danger to the whole community, and to every individual in it; and a danger against which we desire to be protected. That is the case for State education in its very lowest terms.

---

people to abstain from asking such payment. But might not these two impulses work just the opposite way? From the altruistic impulse I am ready to pay for other people, and from the egoistic impulse I want them to pay instead of me.

III. Next let me take the case of the Corn Laws. The end here was the protection of the agricultural interest, but that is the interest of a portion of the community only, and in the last resort the interest of the landlords only (who in England might in those days have been trusted to take care of themselves), at the expense of all the rest of the community. We are all consumers of necessaries; only a fraction of the community are producers of any particular commodity. Thus in this case the end is bad, and we reject legislation of this partial sort. Indeed, we may lay it down as a general maxim, that where economic considerations do not conflict with considerations seriously affecting the physical, intellectual (including æsthetic), and moral welfare of the community, the State will act wisely in adopting a policy of " *laissez faire,*" in abolishing, where possible, laws which interfere with economic causes, and in refusing to introduce such laws. The State may be a better judge of a man's physical, intellectual, or moral interests than the individual himself; it may protect him, to some extent, against disease and danger, compel him to be educated to some extent, and to educate his children; it may remove some strong temptations from him, and insist on an outward decency of conduct, but it cannot be a better judge

(in the long run) of his money interests. It may
protect him against force and fraud, but it cannot
determine better than himself how he should manage
his trade, what price he should pay, and what price
he should ask, whether he should borrow money or
not, and at what interest. Free competition among
producers, free operation of what is called the law of
supply and demand,—*i.e.*, free bargaining between
producer and consumer,—will in the long run lead
to the greatest *production* of wealth, and the greatest
convenience in *exchange*. One cannot add that it will
lead necessarily to the best *distribution* of wealth, because here other than economic considerations come
in. We pass from the abstract science of wealth to the
science of wealth in relation to those ends for which
alone wealth exists. If, in any cases, the principles of
Free Trade have to be deserted, it should be on other
than economic grounds ; it should be because other
considerations are in the particular case so important
as to outweigh the advantage of cheapness of the
particular commodity to the consumer. If free competition is interfered with, it must be because in the
particular case its evils to society are so great as to
outweigh its benefits. I need not linger over the
question of Free Trade, because Mr. Spencer has no
doubts on that subject. I would only point out

that he falls into the very common error of taking
the principle of *laissez faire*, which has proved good
in some cases, as if it were, therefore, applicable in
all.

IV. If we turn from Free Trade to Factory or
Sanitary legislation, we find ourselves face to face
with a very different set of considerations.[1] If
laissez faire in all trade matters is the only policy
which ought to be pursued by a Government that
has heard of economic science, then interferences
with the ordinary course of trade, such as are
involved in the Factory Acts, the Adulteration of
Food Acts and the Public Health Acts, could never
be defended. But they are to be defended, just
because they are interferences where other than
economic considerations come to be more important.
In the case of the Factory Acts, the health and morals
and education of children and young persons, and the

---

[1] Mr. Spencer ignores this difference altogether. Cp. *The
Man versus the State*, p. 49 : " Interferences with the law of
supply and demand, which a generation ago were admitted to
be habitually mischievous, are now being daily made by Acts
of Parliament in new fields." It is the " new fields " that make
all the difference. The champions of Free Trade used unnecessarily wide premises about *laissez faire* which they did not
really prove. Their conclusions we admit, but not their major
premise.

protection of all factory workers against unnecessary danger have been regarded as ends of such importance as to outweigh the inconvenience of interfering with "freedom of contract." Freedom of contract is a taking phrase; but a contract between the capitalist employer, who can afford to wait, and the workman and his family, who must work or starve, is no equal contract. The same may apply, in many cases, to the relation between landlord and tenant. In such cases the State interferes in order to protect those who cannot protect themselves,—a very different thing from professing to direct self-interest where self-interest is quite able to look after itself, or protecting those who are already sufficiently strong against the weak. The Statute of Apprentices and the Factory Acts may both be classed under the abstract head of "interferences with freedom of contract"; but there is an enormous difference between the principle of an Act, which fixed the hours of work for men as twelve hours *at least,* and an Act which limits them for women and young persons to ten hours *at most.* So, again, by legislation against adulteration of food or against insanitary dwellings, the State protects the community against fraud in cases where most persons have neither the time nor the knowledge to protect themselves. Yet such Acts would be artificially classed by Mr. Spencer under the same head with Monopolies, which enabled a privileged few to fatten on the inconvenience or the suffering of the many.

These examples have been purposely chosen from cases where there is a general agreement among Liberals in this country. The underlying principles, on which the expediency or inexpediency of the State intervention in each case is decided, easily admit of further applications—which I may leave to the judicious reader. But, in conclusion, I should like to say just a few words about " Economic Laws," in the name of which practical proposals to remedy acknowledged evils are still exorcised by politicians and newspaper writers, who simply reflect the opinion of those desirous of maintaining the social *status quo.* If by economic laws be meant laws such as the laws of nature, then they are merely statements of what under certain conditions does or would happen ; they are not maxims or precepts telling us what ought to be done. If you jump from the top of the Monument, you will not come down alive ; if you give a person a sufficient quantity of laudanum, he will die ; if there is unchecked economic competition, great social inequality will result from the different economic advantages of different individuals. These three propositions are equally and in the same sense laws of nature, or consequences of such laws. It does not follow that you ought to jump from the top of the Monument, nor that you ought to give any one a large dose of laudanum, nor that there ought to be unchecked competition, unless you wish to kill yourself, or to murder an individual, or to starve a great multitude of human beings, not all of them in every respect the worst of their kind, and possibly capable of sufficient social cohesion to check the individualism of one another and of the doctrinaire politician who preaches *laissez faire* in the name of a misunderstood science with the convenient aid of an ambiguity in language.[1]

---

[1] I am sorry to see that Mr. Raleigh, in the fifth edition of his useful *Elementary Politics*, continues to employ the mischievous phrase, " the political creed of those who still believe in economic laws" (p. 156). I call it mischievous because it conceals a step in the argument, and illegitimately claims the sanction of science for *laissez faire*. A man may believe an economic law—*i.e.*, hold it to be true ; he cannot be said, strictly, to believe *in* it, though he may believe in some practical policy based on his belief that such and such is the case. Let us hope that Professor Marshall's words will become an accepted dogma, even among " orthodox" economists who may happen also to be individualist politicians : " The Laws of Economics are statements of tendencies expressed in the indicative mood, and not ethical precepts in the imperative." (*Principles of Economics*, Pref. p. vi. Cp. p. 89.)

IV.

THE POLITICAL PHILOSOPHY OF
THOMAS HILL GREEN.

§ I. POLITICAL PHILOSOPHY IN ENGLAND.

IN no country has there been through many centuries a more continuous discussion of the questions of practical politics than in England. In no country has the interest in politics been diffused more widely through the whole community. But there has been no corresponding activity in the philosophical study of the nature of society and the State. Hobbes and Herbert Spencer are almost the only two English philosophers who have treated politics as an integral part of a complete philosophical system: and it might be shown that the monarchical prejudices of Hobbes and the individualist prejudices of Spencer have hindered them from even so adequate a treatment of the nature of the State as their philosophical theories admitted.[1] We can hardly reckon the brilliant political Essays of Hume in this connection, for Hume was professedly a destroyer of systems, and his attention to politics and to history went

---

[1] With regard to Mr. Spencer see Essay I.

along with his despair of metaphysics. The political writings of Locke and of John Stuart Mill have not only a permanent interest for the student of political ideas, but have exercised in different ways a direct influence on the course of political events; but this influence was direct, very much because both Locke and Mill wrote on politics more as politicians than as philosophers. Locke makes no explicit link between his theory of knowledge and his theory of government, though both were given to the world about the same time; in fact, the ideas of a "law of nature" and "natural rights," on which his political doctrines rest, belong to that manner of thinking which the analytic method of the *Essay* contributed in the long run to discredit. Hume attacked the idea of "social contract" by using just such weapons as Locke had used in attacking "innate ideas." In the case of Mill the careful reader can trace the connection between the psychical atomism (for he treats sensations as if they were psychical atoms) which forms the fundamental assumption in his theory of knowledge and the individualism out of which his practical interest in human well-being helped him partially to escape; but, though Mill himself was fully aware of the ultimate interdependence of different departments of human thought and human prejudice, and though

he regarded himself as fighting for the same cause of
progress in his *Logic* and *Examination of Hamilton*
on the one hand, and in his *Liberty* and *Representative Government* on the other, yet the two sets of
works are obviously addressed to different classes of
readers, and it requires the diligence of the student
to see more than a biographical connection ; and, in
any case, Mill was concerned with practical questions
about the limits of government-action and the
arrangement of representative bodies, not with the
primary and more strictly philosophical questions
about the nature of the State. In fact, the intense
preoccupation of the most vigorous English minds
in the immediately practical problems of legislation
and administration has diverted attention from an
investigation of the ultimate principles on which
government is based. And, while it has been an
enormous advantage that those amongst us who have
written about government have themselves had some
practical acquaintance with what legislation and
administration mean, we have lost something, not
only in clearness of theory but in consistency and
firmness of practice, because the elementary terms
of political discussion have passed current without
having their value scientifically tested. In Germany,
on the other hand, some of the very best energy of

philosophical thinking has been devoted to the doctrine of rights and the nature and functions of the State ; but, owing to the fact that political liberty is not yet very well known in Germany, we may occasionally complain (echoing the complaint of Aristotle) that the Sophists, or Professors, who profess to teach πολιτική, or Staatslehre, have no practical experience of their subject, while the practical politicians of our own country have not raised their knowledge of the State from the domain of experience to that of thought.

This scarcity of English political philosophy gives a peculiar importance to the portion of the late Professor Green's *Philosophical Works,* which contains his "Lectures on the Principles of Political Obligation." [1] The same metaphysical subtlety, which had been already applied to the Theory of Knowledge and the Theory of Ethics, is here directed to a criticism of political theories and to the attempt thereby to arrive at a more adequate doctrine of political rights

---

[1] *Works* of Thomas Hill Green, late Fellow of Balliol College, and Whyte's Professor of Moral Philosophy in the University of Oxford. Edited by R. L. Nettleship, Fellow of Balliol College, Oxford. Vol. II. London : Longmans. 1886. (See pp. 308–the end.) These *Lectures* were published separately in 1895.

and obligations. To those who knew Professor Green personally, this part of his *Works* has an additional and very special significance ; for here we have the meeting-point between the speculative and the practical interests, which to onlookers might seem to be two divergent channels in which his life ran, but which in his own mind were united and tended in the same direction. The painstaking pursuit of philosophical truth and the endeavour in all things to be the good citizen and the honest politician were equally characteristic of the man, and sprang from a common source of earnestness and sincerity. His conscience was equally exacting in speculation and in practice. His philosophical thinking was to him no mere exercise of intellectual ingenuity, but provided the basis of his conduct and influenced the details of his actions to an extent very rare even amongst those whom we consider the most conscientious of men. He neither despised the small matters of local politics, nor forgot the wider interests of mankind. He went straight from the declaration of the poll, when he was elected a town councillor, to lecture on *The Critique of Pure Reason.* He was robbed of his sleep by thinking about the Eastern Question, and dreading lest the country should be driven, by motives "of which perhaps a diffused desire for excitement has been the most innocent,"[1] into what he regarded as an indefensible and un-righteous war. His strong opinions on the liquor traffic were in his own mind directly connected with his conception of the ethical end and the nature of rights.

§ 2. THE RELATION BETWEEN PHILOSOPHY AND POLITICS.

The late Mark Pattison [2] thought it must have been due to "a certain puzzle-headedness" on the part of the Professor that he, "a staunch Liberal," should have imported into Oxford " an *à priori* philosophy, which under various disguises aims at exempting Man from the order of nature, and making him into a unique being whose organism is not to be subject to the uniform laws which govern all other Being that is known to us." It was, in any case, from no want of thinking and puzzling over problems, that Pro-fessor Green was at once "a staunch Liberal" and an "*à priori* philosopher." Mark Pattison's phrase, "*exempting* Man from the order of Nature," must be challenged on behalf alike of Kant and Green, who

---

[1] Cp. *Philosophical Works*, ii. p. 476.
[2] See his *Memoirs*, pp. 167, 242.

by no means deny that Man is a part of Nature, and
that human actions are natural events, but who do
deny that Man can be understood if he be considered
as *merely* a part of Nature and his actions *merely* as
natural events. But that question must be left for
the present.

There is a remarkable passage in the *Autobiography*
of J. S. Mill (pp. 273–275), where he says :—

"The difference between these two schools of philosophy,
that of Intuition and that of Experience and Association,
is not a mere matter of abstract speculation ; it is full of
practical consequences, and lies at the foundation of all the
greatest differences of practical opinion in an age of progress.
The practical reformer has continually to demand that changes
be made in things which are supported by powerful and widely
spread feelings, or to question the apparent necessity and
indefeasibleness of established facts ; and it is often an indis-
pensable part of his argument to show, how those powerful
feelings had their origin, and how those facts came to seem
necessary and indefeasible. There is therefore a natural
hostility between him and a philosophy which discourages the
explanation of feelings and moral facts by circumstances and
association, and prefers to treat them as ultimate elements of
human nature ; a philosophy which is addicted to holding up
favourite doctrines as intuitive truths, and deems intuition to be
the voice of Nature and of God, speaking with an authority
higher than that of our reason. In particular, I have long felt
that the prevailing tendency to regard all the marked distinctions
of human character as innate, and in the main indelible, and to
ignore the irresistible proofs that by far the greater part of those

differences, whether between individuals, races, or sexes, are
such as not only might but naturally would be produced by
differences in circumstances, is one of the chief hindrances to
the rational treatment of great social questions, and one of the
greatest stumbling-blocks to human improvement. This tendency has its source in the intuitional metaphysics which
characterised the reaction of the nineteenth century against the
eighteenth, and it is a tendency so agreeable to human indolence,
as well as to conservative interests generally, that unless attacked
at the very root, it is sure to be carried to even a greater length
than is really justified by the more moderate forms of the
intuitional philosophy. That philosophy, not always in its
moderate forms, had ruled the thought of Europe for the greater
part of a century. My Father's Analysis of the Mind, my
own Logic, and Professor Bain's great treatise, had attempted
to re-introduce a better mode of philosophising, latterly with
quite as much success as could be expected ; but I had for
some time felt that the mere contrast of the two philosophies
was not enough, that there ought to be a hand-to-hand fight
between them, that controversial as well as expository writings
were needed, and that the time was come when such controversy
would be useful."

These considerations Mill assigns as his special reason
for attacking Sir William Hamilton.

Sir William Hamilton was a Whig, it is true (and
a Whig in those days was still a Liberal) ; but undoubtedly the doctrine of "intuitive truths" has
served as a convenient formula under which time-
honoured delusions and abuses have been sheltered
from the attacks of critical analysis and reforming

zeal. The "intuitional metaphysics" of this country and the so-called "spiritualist" philosophy, which flourished in France under the restored monarchy, have both been associated with the maintenance of existing ideas and institutions in society, politics, and religion. The supporters of these Intuitionalist systems very often pointed to the triumphs of the Kantian Criticism and sometimes of the post-Kantian Idealism in Germany, glad to use the sanction of great names where they were available, without committing themselves to speculative theories which had the reputation of being vaguely "dangerous." Those, too, who first introduced the names and theories of the German philosophers were generally enlisted on the side of the reaction against the French Revolution—Coleridge most conspicuously, De Quincey and others following in the same line. In Thomas Love Peacock's *Nightmare Abbey* the "Kantian" philosopher, Mr. Flosky, is represented as an extreme obscurantist reactionary; his very name, by an old-fashioned etymology, signifying "the lover of darkness." Certainly Hegel was a Prussian Conservative, and Schelling seemed to lead the way through mysticism back into the fold of the Catholic Church ; but people would appear to have forgotten how the aged Kant, with tears in his eyes,

said his *Nunc dimittis* on hearing of the proclamation
of the French Republic, and how Fichte was the
intellectual father of German Socialism. Mill and
Pattison might also have remembered that Hobbes
was an Absolutist, and that Hume became more and
more a Tory without becoming less a sceptic ; and
it has not yet been explicitly proved that there is a
logical connection between " philosophic doubt " and
support of the Tory party. From a man's philosophical speculations we cannot always predict his
attitude in practical politics. But the mistake in the
statements both of Mill and Pattison lies in the
assumption that the *à priori* philosophy of Kant
and his followers is identical with the " intuitional
metaphysics " which had been the familiar object of
attack to the English Empiricists. The resemblance
between the answers to Hume of Kant and of Reid
is slight and superficial, compared with the difference between them. And the attitude of Hegel to
the problems of knowledge and of life is distinct
both from the old metaphysics and from the new
empiricism. The German Idealist is equally dis-
tasteful to the defender of " innate ideas " or " intuitive
truths " and to their assailant—because he is apt to
be misunderstood by both. And, if we pass to the
more practical application of philosophy, there would

be more reason for classing Hegel and his followers along with Comte than with the obscurantist theologians whom Pattison disliked and the obstructionist Conservatives whom Mill opposed. Comte, it is true, presents a double face: he is both of the Revolution and against it. And the same remark really applies to Hegel. Hence it is no wonder that opposite parties should have started from the same great school, and that Catholic and Positivist, Conservative and Socialist should have found weapons in the same armoury. Which is the truer interpreter it is of course important to decide ; and it does not always follow that the initiator of new ideas will himself be the best judge of their practical tendency.

Another side to the mistake in Pattison's remark about Green is the failure to appreciate fully the change that has come over English Liberalism. During the eighteenth century and the earlier part of the nineteenth century, the friends of social and political reform were engaged in a struggle mainly against mischievous interference with individual liberty on the part of a government which chiefly represented the influence and interests of a hereditary ruling class: thus Liberalism came to be identified with the criticism and removal of repressive laws and institutions, and an intellectual basis for such a policy was naturally found in a philosophy of critical analysis. It was in the same spirit that Locke, the father of English Empiricism, criticised the doctrine of innate ideas and the doctrine of the divine right of kings. And this alliance between Empiricism in philosophy and Liberalism in politics continued with few exceptions to the time of John Stuart Mill, whose philosophical creed remained, on the whole, in its intellectual aspects what his father had taught him, however modified by emotional sympathies, but whose political ideas underwent a greater change than he himself was aware of. The efforts of Liberals having passed from the merely negative work of removing mischievous State-action to the more positive task of employing the power of a government, which is now, more or less, the real representative of the " general will," in behalf of the well-being of the community, it is natural and necessary that the intellectual basis of the new political creed should be found in a philosophy of construction, and not in one of merely negative criticism and analysis. Thus there is a real affinity between the newer stages of Radicalism and a political philosophy such as that of Hegel or of Comte, apart from the special influence of Prussian bureaucracy in the one case and the admiration for mediæval Catholicism in the other, which are, after all, elements belonging more to the idiosyncrasy of the philosophers than to the essence of the ideas of which they are the most notable representatives.

§ 3. KANT AND ARISTOTLE.—THE ETHICAL END.

These remarks must not, however, be taken as implying that Professor Green was only "the importer" (to adopt Mark Pattison's phrase) of a German philosophy. It is rather common to hear him classed as one of "the English school of Hegelians." He would certainly not have acknowledged the title himself, and it is really inaccurate—unless it be very carefully qualified. If we are to connect him with any particular names of philosophers, it would be least misleading to say that he corrected Kant by Aristotle and Aristotle by Kant. Now, this is just what might have been said of Hegel himself; for, if Hegel had no other claims to distinction, he would have this, that first of modern philosophers he really understood and appreciated the Greeks. Referring to Hegel, Green is reported to have said, "It must all be done over again"—*i.e.* he admitted the general validity of Hegel's objections to the subjective, and, in appearance, merely

psychological method of Kant, and to the survivals
(from the old metaphysics) in Kant's system of ways
of thinking and speaking, of which Kant himself
had implicitly made an end ; but he considered the
Hegelian attempt to read off the whole secret of
the Universe, to fill up the whole contents of the
eternal Self-consciousness, premature and over-hasty,
and he set himself to do some small part of the
vast work in a more modest spirit and with special
reference to the English theories which he found
occupying the field.[1]

There is a brief reference to Greek philosophy in
the lectures on Political Obligation (§ 39), where
it is said that, just because Plato and Aristotle
regarded man as finding his end in the end of the
State, they laid the foundation for a true theory
of rights.　In the *Prolegomena to Ethics* it was
argued that Greek ethics were defective, not in
defining the end as self-satisfaction or self-realisation
($\dot{\epsilon}\nu\dot{\epsilon}\rho\gamma\epsilon\iota\alpha\ \psi\upsilon\chi\hat{\eta}s$), but because, in the stage of moral

---

[1] It is worth calling attention to the very great degree in
which the questions discussed and the phraseology adopted
in the "Lectures on Political Obligation" are determined by
Locke's *Treatise of Civil Government.*　Green's polemic against
Locke's theory of knowledge has not prevented his sympathy
with the most *politically* important English book on the nature
of government.

and social progress then attained, this self-realisation
was only possible to a few, and so here it is said :
"Practically it is only the Greek man that Aristotle
regards as φύσει πολίτης, but the Greek conception
of citizenship once established was applicable to all
men capable of a common interest." As Aristotle
concludes his " Ethics " by passing on to Politics,
because the good life can only be fully realised by
the citizen of the good State, so Green's view of
Ethics is completed by his view of Politics ; because
he conceives that the function of the State is to make
it possible for men to realise themselves, which they
can only do by attaining a good that is a common
good. In the ethical writings the phrase " self-
satisfaction " or " self-realisation " is perhaps the
more conspicuous, in the political " common good "
(which, however, is used quite as much in the
ethical) ; but it is just because to Green these terms
are identical expressions of the end for man that
his ethics can escape the reproach of being only
the Egoistic Hedonism he professedly rejected come
back under a disguised form. "If the end be self-
realisation," it might be objected, "does it not depend
entirely on the individual what he chooses to do?
The pleasure-seeker might say he was realising
himself quite as much as the patriot or the philan-

thropist, and how can you prove him wrong?" He can only be proved wrong, if it be shown that the self in a human being is something other than a mere series of feelings, and so in its true nature other than a mere subject for pleasurable sensations. And Green argues that the self is other than a mere series of feelings just because it is what renders possible the consciousness of a series of feelings : the self-consciousness, which is manifested in them, must yet be other than they ; for, as J. S. Mill himself had seen, it was a "paradox" that what is only a series of feelings should be aware of itself as a series.[1] In this fact of self-consciousness, discovered by examination of mental phenomena, Green finds the metaphysical basis of Ethics ; on the other side, the interpretation of self-realisation as the realisation of a common good is what makes the connection between Ethics and Politics. "The good which a man seeks for himself is not a succession of pleasures, but objects which, when realised, are permanent contributions to a social good which thus satisfies the permanent self."[2] Thus, the practical tests which Green applies to determine the rightness of any

---

[1] Cp. Mill's *Examination of Hamilton*, p. 248 (5th edition).
[2] *Prolegomena to Ethics*, § 234 (Analysis).

proposed course of conduct, either for the individual
or for the State, seem to coincide with those which
would be proposed by the Utilitarian. Of this he is
quite aware,[1] but he considers that he has a logical
justification for applying the test of social well-being
to which the Utilitarian, with his Hedonist starting-
point, has no claim, and that, having defined the end
as the realisation of a permanent self-satisfaction,
he escapes the difficulties attending the balancing of
pleasures and pains. The practical benefits conferred
by Utilitarianism on political and social conduct he
is most ready to acknowledge, but he maintains that
the significant part of Bentham's famous formula was
not "the greatest happiness," but the reference to
the greatest number, and especially the added clause,
" Every one to count for one and no one for more
than one." [2] This he holds to have been the main
source both of the beneficence and of the unpopu-
larity of Utilitarianism. " The healthful influence of
Utilitarianism has arisen from its giving a wider and
more impartial range to the desire to do good, not

---

[1] Cf. "Lectures on Political Obligation" (in *Philosophical
Works*, vol. ii.), § 23, of which Mr. Nettleship's analysis is :—
"The utilitarian theory so far agrees with that here advocated
that it grounds existing law, not on a 'natural' law prior to it,
but on an end which it serves."

[2] *Prolegomena to Ethics*, § 213.

from its stimulating that desire." [1] When we look
to politics rather than to ethics, we shall see the
reason why Green would have found himself, in the
case of so many questions, on the same platform
with John Stuart Mill, and that without the least
sacrifice of philosophical consistency. He would
have agreed with a follower of Locke or of Rousseau
in demanding, for instance, an extension of the
franchise ; but he would have agreed with Bentham
and Mill in objecting to any talk about "natural
rights :" he would have preferred to put the matter
on the ground of social expediency. But while Mill
would *ultimately* have brought the question back to
some consideration of pleasures and pains, Green
would have insisted that the social expediency was
determined ultimately, not by the probable effects
on the greatest number of pleasures of an individual
consistently with those of other individuals, but by
the scope given to the individual for exercising
all his capacities of self-development, all true self-
development implying, however, the well-being of a
community ; for man, as we often repeat without
fully understanding what we say, is essentially "a
social animal." The convenience of Bentham's

---

[1] *Prolegomena to Ethics*, § 331 (Anal.).

formula is the readiness with which it supplies a means of checking and criticising individual and class prejudice and selfishness. And formulæ for ordinary rough use need not be philosophically unassailable. There is no reason why the Idealist, after making clear his objections to Hedonism, should not join hands with the Utilitarian. In fact, an ethical system like Green's is really, on its practical side, J. S. Mill's Utilitarianism with a securer basis and a criterion provided, which Mill cannot logically provide, for distinguishing the different *qualities* of pleasures. Mill, we know, would himself prefer the higher pleasures. But what justifies him in considering those to be the best pleasures for other people? To say that the common good is the end may *seem* more vague than to say that pleasure is the end ; but to say that pleasure is the end is in reality quite as vague and is more open to objection, because the vagueness is less obvious, and therefore more misleading.

§ 4. " FREEDOM "—NEGATIVE AND POSITIVE.

Besides "self-realisation" and a "common good" as phrases for the ethical, which is also ultimately the political end, Green is willing to allow Hegel's

L

term "freedom." In a special discussion of the "different senses of 'freedom' as applied to will and to the moral progress of man,"[1] which may be taken as intermediate between the *Prolegomena to Ethics* and the Political Lectures, he distinguishes between a *generic* sense of "freedom," in which it applies to *all* will—whatever be the character of the object willed ("freedom" meaning, simply, self-determination or acting on preference)—and a *particular* sense, according to which acts are only "free" in so far as the self-realising principle in man tends to be realised— *i.e.*, in so far as the objects of reason and of will tend to coincide.[2] Free acts are rational acts. In this sense Hegel's dictum, that the object of the State is freedom, is accepted, but only as the statement of an ideal to which actual States, so far as they are well regulated, tend to approximate.

"Hegel's account of freedom as realised in the State does not seem to correspond to the facts of society as it is, or even as under the alterable conditions of human nature, it ever could be; though undoubtedly there is a work of moral liberation, which society, through its various agencies, is constantly carrying on for the individual."[3]

---

[1] See *Philosophical Works*, vol. ii. pp. 308–333.

[2] Cp. Spinoza's use of *libertas* as equivalent to the rule of reason, *potentia intellectus*.

[3] *Philosophical Works*, ii. p. 314.

Now it is obvious that freedom in this sense as the ideal end of the State is very different from the "freedom" to which Locke considered that man had a "natural right" in which a well-managed State ought to secure him.[1] This freedom is the mere negative freedom of being left alone, and corresponds to the generic sense of freedom in morals. It is a mere means to the attainment of the freedom which is itself an end. This distinction shows what Green's attitude to the questions about State-action and *laissez faire* was likely to be. State-action, he holds, is expedient just in so far as it tends to promote "freedom" in the sense of self-determined action directed to the objects of reason, inexpedient so far as it tends to interfere with this. The direct legal enforcement of morality cannot be considered expedient or inexpedient : it is *impossible.* The morality of an act depends on the state of the will of the agent, and therefore the act done under compulsion ceases to have the character of a moral act. It wants the negative con-

---

[1] Locke, however, sees that the freedom which means "being left alone by other individuals" does not mean "being left alone by the State." He at least is free from the delusion that the equal freedom of all can be obtained by an absence of legislation. See the passages quoted in *note* on p. 85. above.

dition of morality.[1] But on the other hand, there is
no *à priori* presumption in favour of a general policy
of *laissez faire*, because in a vast number of cases
the individual does not find himself in a position in
which he can act "freely" (*i.e.*, direct his action to
objects which reason assigns as desirable) without
the intervention of the State to put him in such a
position—*e.g.*, by ensuring that he shall have at least
some education. Terms like "freedom," "compulsion," "interference," are very apt to be misleading.
As Green points out, "'compulsory education' need
not be 'compulsory,' except to those who have no
spontaneity to be deadened:" and it is "not as a
purely moral duty on the part of a parent, but as the
prevention of a hindrance to the capacity for rights
on the part of children, that education should be en-
forced by the State."[2] The "interference" may be
interference in behalf of individual liberty—even in
the negative sense of liberty. So also, when interference with "freedom of contract" is spoken of, we

---

[1] The same holds, of course, with regard to religion, if religion
is anything more than ritual observance. There is a story that
some Tory Churchman (who must have been born two centuries
too late) said to the late Professor Thorold Rogers: "Religion
must be compulsory, or else there will be no religion at all."
"I cannot see the difference," was the answer.

[2] Lectures on Political Obligation, § 209.

must consider not only those who are interfered with, but those whose freedom is increased by that interference.[1]

It would be out of place here to give a detailed account of the way in which Green works out his own theory of political obligation and doctrine of rights by a criticism of Hobbes, Spinoza, Locke, Rousseau, and Austin—a criticism which is probably more valuable and suggestive than any dogmatic treatise on political science. The foregoing exposition may, at least, serve to make it clear that, whether Professor Green was mistaken or not in his development of Kantian and Aristotelian philosophy, or in his sympathy with Radical politics, he was at least thoroughly and perfectly consistent. The State has, in his view, not the mere policeman's business of stepping in to arrest the wrongdoer, not the sole function of ruthlessly enforcing fulfilment of contracts, whatever these contracts may be and between whomsoever made ; but the duty of providing such an environment for individual men and women as to

---

[1] There is a popular lecture of Prof. Green's on *Liberal Legislation and Freedom of Contract*, published by Slatter & Rose, Oxford, 1881, republished in *Works*, vol. iii. pp. 365–386. The philosophical doctrines of the College lectures will be found to underlie the popular lecture, which serves as an excellent commentary on them.

give *all*, as far as possible, an equal chance of realising what is best in their intellectual and moral
natures. Material well-being *alone* might hinder,
instead of furthering, this end ; but we need not be
afraid of weakening moral responsibility by making
a moral and *human* life possible to those for whom
at present it is practically hopeless. The politician
is thus not inconsistent, who, after opposing all such
State-action as "tended to strengthen some at the
cost of others' weakness," supports such measures of
compulsion as shall secure to all, as far as possible,
true freedom—*i.e.*, "a positive power or capacity of
doing or enjoying something worth doing or enjoying, and that, too, something that we do or enjoy
in common with others."[1] No better expression of
Professor Green's social ideal can be found than in
words of his that have already been quoted as typical
by Professor Caird :—

"I confess to hoping for a time when the phrase ['the
education of a gentleman'] will have lost its meaning, because
the sort of education which alone makes the gentleman in any
true sense will be within the reach of all. As it was the aspira-
tion of Moses that all the Lord's people should be prophets, so
with all seriousness and reverence we may hope and pray for a

---

[1] *Liberal Legislation and Freedom of Contract*, p. 9. (*Works*,
vol. iii. p. '371.)

condition of English society, in which all honest citizens will recognise themselves and be recognised by each other as gentlemen." [1]

This is certainly a democratic, some would call it a Socialist, sentiment. It is only one outcome of the recognition that the ethical end of self-realisation is an end for all human beings, and that we must get rid of those barriers of class and caste which we are in the habit of saying that Christianity has broken down.

---

[1] *The Work to be done by the new Oxford High School:* A Lecture addressed to the Wesleyan Literary Society, Dec. 19, 1881. (*Works,* vol. iii. p. 475.)

APPENDIX.

NOTE A.

THE DISTINCTION BETWEEN SOCIETY AND THE STATE.

THIS distinction is generally assumed as if there were no doubt as to its reality and its value; but it has, I think, been far too little discussed and examined. There is an admirable short paper on the subject by Mr. J. S. Mann in Vol. I., No. 3, pp. 92–98 of the *Proceedings of the Aristotelian Society.* "The antithesis of State and Society," says Mr. Mann,—"first, I believe, formulated by Hegel, and now a commonplace of German writers on Statsrecht and Ethik—touches on actual political questions in more points than any other doctrine to be found in their works." "The State arises," he adds further on, "according to Hegel, from Society, to ensure that the individual shall be fully realised, chiefly through his own conscious action. The State guarantees him his individuality, which Society with its self-seeking struggle of competitors tends to efface." It will be obvious that this is the opinion about the function of the State which I have tried to vindicate in these essays. More than to any other man we owe this sounder political philosophy to Hegel, whose influence pervades the thinking of many who are quite unconscious of it, and even of some who are in the habit of reviling his name. I do not mean, of course, that this conception of the State is in any sense peculiar to Hegel (if it were, he might be an "original thinker," but he would not be the typical philosopher of his age); but simply that he has given the completest expression to that organic conception of human society which has begun to free political theory and practice from the narrowness and false abstractions of the individualist philosophers of the seventeenth and eighteenth centuries.

Mr. Mann holds that the antithesis has a purely regulative or subjective value (like the conceptions of abstract political economy), but no objective or historical reality. How then did this antithesis, which seems so conspicuously absent from the writings of Plato and Aristotle, come to be so prominent as it is in our modern way of thinking and speaking? "May it be suggested," says Mr. Mann, "that Hegel's conception of the antithesis is partly reminiscent of the Social Contract, partly due to the circumstances of Germany in his time? In Prussia there were definitely marked orders or 'estates,'" etc. Now this latter suggestion suggests a good deal more. But what I am going to say as to the historical genesis of the distinction must be taken as purely tentative.

The antithesis, I have said, is conspicuously absent from the writings of Plato and Aristotle. With respect to Aristotle, a slight qualification must be made. In distinguishing "Œconomics" (the science of household-management) from "Politics," Aristotle has given the starting-point for the antithesis: for his discussion of Œconomics in *Politics*, Book I., deals with many subjects which we should not put under the rubric "Family." The "social and economic" questions of slavery, hired labour, property, etc., fall under his science of "Œconomics," and are treated of apart from and preliminary to the main subjects of Politics. Aristotle's conservatism, moreover, leads him to save the family and private property from the absorption and annihilation they undergo in Plato's ideal state, in which there is no social institution that is not a political institution. Nevertheless, when Aristotle comes to sketch out his own "best state" (a sketch indeed that is, in all probability, unfinished), we find him mainly occupied with "social" questions, such as health, marriage, education, etc. : as to political organisation he has comparatively little to say. Take along with this his opposition to the "Sophistic" theory that the State has no moral functions, but has only to protect individual rights (*Pol.* III. 9, § 8), and we see that in the famous sentence, "Man is by nature a *political* animal," something very much more is meant by "political" than suggests itself at once to the modern ear. In the *De Regimine Principum* which has come down to us among the works of Thomas Aquinas, and the first book of which (along with part of the second) is generally accepted as his, the equivalent of this Aristotelian dictum is to be found in the words, "homo est animal *sociale et politicum*" (in his *Commentary on the Politics* Thomas Aquinas writes "civile et domesticum"). Is not this insertion of "sociale" alongside of "politicum" significant of the different way in which the State presented itself to the mind of the Greek and to the mind of the medieval philosopher?

Now where are we to look for an explanation of this

difference save in the effects of the Roman Empire? The Romans "devoured and broke in pieces" the states of the old world, and through the long centuries of the *pax Romana* we may say that within the wide limits of the Empire there existed Society without the State, except as a "negatively regulative" institution. Citizenship, when made co-extensive with the Roman world, had no longer any political meaning: it gave only certain legal and social privileges. The State would appear to the individual as merely the machinery for defending Society against the aggression of barbarians from without, and for maintaining order and enforcing contracts within. When Western Europe began, with the help of the Roman Church, to emerge from the chaos into which the downfall of the Empire had thrown it, in that curious combination of archaic barbarian usage and late Roman law, which resulted in Feudalism, Society found itself arranged in certain more or less definite castes, which, for illustration's sake, I may describe as horizontal layers; the vertical divisions which mark off one nation from another were as yet faint and ill-defined compared with some of the horizontal dividing lines. Thus the clergy, with their Latin tongue, had more in common with one another than with the laity of their own particular country; and "clergy" in the early middle ages meant almost the entire brain-working population. A medieval university was a cosmopolitan, not a national institution. To a less extent the same would hold of the nobility. The nobles of different countries had more in common with one another than with the clergy or commons of their own land. They might fight with one another, it is true; but they did that often enough, even though they had sworn allegiance to the same king. A fight to them was just like a disputation to the clergy: it did not interrupt a general community of caste feeling. The noble of one country could marry the noble of another more easily than a commoner of his own. (Contrast the Greek tendency to forbid marriage with aliens.) The *Almanach de Gotha* represents a modern survival of this international social layer. The horizontal lines in the lower social strata were in medieval times less continuous, and the vertical lines relatively more distinct; but so soon as trade and commerce began to rise again, their international character showed itself in spite of State action (hostile tariffs, differences of currency, etc.), and has grown continuously till, at the present time, to the banking and commercial community, nationality is chiefly a matter of accident or convenience. The partners in the same business may purposely make themselves citizens of different nations. Lastly, the international solidarity of labour has first become conscious of itself in the present century. The "nationality movement" has, indeed, culminated in this age; but it began very long ago. England, geographically fortunate, felt itself a united nation in the earlier middle ages, France in the later. Germany at the beginning of this century was one Society, arranged in class layers, but many "States." The French Revolution proclaimed fraternity, but its immediate consequence was an intensification of national feeling. Instead of breaking through the vertical lines it made them more distinct; and now, at length, we have again many nations which are the equivalents of

Greek city-states. And as of old, Society and State tend to coincide, political questions to become identical with social questions.

Does this mean, as in ancient Hellas, a perpetuation of strife between rival states? The outlook is not hopeful, but neither is it hopeless; for the modern "nationality movement" has been democratic, and the very class which now makes the State become social or "socialistic" is also the class which begins to feel its international solidarity the most.

But it is impossible to write a philosophy of history in a brief note, and I must avoid the dangerous region of prophecy. I only suggest that the growth of national (State) feeling, since it is the very thing which has put an end to popular jealousy of State action, is itself a valuable step in the transition to something beyond the "natural" state of war between nation and nation. The several nations have had to become conscious of themselves by antagonism; but the moment the nationality question is settled, the social question appears and produces a new feeling of common interest among the larger part of the population—a feeling which may be expected, in time, to lead to the growth of wider and higher political ideals than those of nationalities based on narrow prejudices of race (or supposed race), religion, or traditional hatred.

Note B.

THE CONCEPTION OF SOVEREIGNTY.

There is a passage in Locke's *Treatise of Civil Government*, Book II., ch. xiii., which seems to me to suggest a more satisfactory theory of Sovereignty than is to be found elsewhere :—

"Though in a constituted commonwealth, standing upon its own basis, and acting according to its own nature, that is, acting for the preservation of the community, there can be but one supreme power, which is the legislative, to which all the rest are and must be subordinate, yet the legislative being only a fiduciary power to act for certain ends, there remains still in the people a supreme power to remove or alter the legislative when they find the legislative act contrary to the trust reposed in them ; for all power given with trust for the attaining an end being limited by that end, whenever that end is manifestly neglected or opposed, the trust must necessarily be forfeited, and the power devolve into the hands of those that gave it, who may place it anew where they shall think best for their safety and security. And thus the community perpetually retains a supreme power of saving themselves from the attempts and designs of anybody, even of their legislators, whenever they shall be so foolish or so wicked as to lay and carry on designs against the liberties and properties of the subject ; for no man or society of men, having a power to deliver up their preservation, or consequently the means of it to the absolute will and arbitrary dominion of another, whenever any one shall go about to bring them into such a slavish condition, they will always have a right to preserve what they have not a power to part with ; and to rid themselves of those who invade this fundamental, sacred and unalterable law of self-preservation for which they entered into society ; and thus the community may be said in this respect to be always the supreme power, but not as considered under any form of government, because this power of the people can never take place till the government be dissolved.

In all cases whilst the government subsists, the legislative is the supreme power ; for what can give laws to another must needs be superior to him, and since the legislative is no otherwise legislative of the society but by the right it has to make laws for all the parts and for every member of the society, prescribing rules to their actions, and giving power of execution where they are transgressed, the legislative must needs be the supreme, and all other powers in any members or parts of the society derived from and subordinate to it.

In some commonwealths where the legislative is not always in being, and the executive is vested in a single person, who has also a share in the legislative, there that single person in a very tolerable sense may also be called supreme, not that he has in himself all the supreme power, which is that of law-making, but because he has in him the supreme execution from whom all inferior magistrates derive all their several subordinate powers, or at least the greatest part of them ; having also no legislative superior to him, there being no law to be made without his consent which cannot be expected should ever subject him to the other part of the legislative, he is properly enough in this sense supreme. But yet it is to be observed, that though oaths of allegiance and fealty are taken to him, it is not to him as supreme legislator, but as supreme executor of the law, made by a joint power of him with others, allegiance being nothing but obedience according to law, which when he violates, he has no right to obedience, nor can claim it otherwise than as the public person vested with the power of the law, and so is to be considered as the image, phantom, or representative of the commonwealth, acted by the will of the society, declared in its laws ; and thus he has no will, no power but that of the law. But when he quits this representation, this public will, and acts by his own private will, he degrades himself, and is but a single private person without power, and without will that has any right to obedience ; the members owing no obedience but to the public will of the society."

In this passage Locke is obviously thinking of the English Constitution as he interpreted it, and wished it to be, and as the Revolution of 1688 practically made it. He distinguishes three senses in which we may speak of the sovereign or "supreme power" in the independent political society to which we belong.

(1) There is, first of all, what he mentions last, the sovereign power ascribed to the constitutional monarch whom we call "our most gracious sovereign," etc. (2) There is the supreme law-making body in the commonwealth, that body behind which the lawyer *quâ* lawyer does not go. This is the sovereign in the sense of Austin's apologists at the present day (*e.g.*, Mr. F. Harrison, Art. on "The English School of Jurisprudence" in *Fortnightly Review*, Vol. xxx., 1878). But Austin himself goes behind the supreme law-making body to the persons who appoint a portion of it. Sir G. C. Lewis more cautiously abides by the lawyer's view of the constitution, according to which sovereignty resides in the Parliament (*i.e.*, according to the lawyer's, as distinct from the historian's, use of that term, in King, Lords, and the House of Commons). For the lawyer *quâ* lawyer a law is "good law," though it were made by a parliament which had entirely lost the confidence of the electorate, and was legislating in direct defiance of the express understanding on which the majority of the elected portion of it had been returned. If Austin's account of sovereignty were an account of the legal (I mean the lawyer's) sovereign, the Septennial Act would be bad law, because it was passed by a House of Commons elected under the Triennial Act. (3) Locke recognises that behind the legislature there is, not merely the electorate, but the whole mass of public opinion and the whole physical force of the

people. This "supreme power that remains still in the people " may not manifest itself conspicuously, except in the case of a successful revolution ; but this is the real ultimate political sovereign in an independent political society. In recognising this, Locke is in entire agreement with his follower Rousseau, whose "inalienable sovereignty of the people " is identical with Locke's "supreme power that remains still in the people." And it is a conception that continues perfectly valid, though we brush away the idea of "natural rights," as being anything more than (1), the might or power, moral *and* physical, residing in any body of persons, or (2) whatever, in the private opinion of any one using the phrase, a well regulated society *ought* to secure to its individual members. It is the fashion in England to laud Locke and revile Rousseau. Rousseau is a clear writer, and Locke is not. Rousseau wrote before a violent revolution, and Locke published his book after a very quiet one. These are the main differences between them.

It would be convenient to name these "three sovereigns" in such a way as to make the distinction fit other forms of government than the British Constitution. I propose therefore to distinguish them as (1) the *nominal* (2) the *legal* (3) the ultimate *political* sovereigns. By (1) the *nominal* sovereign, I mean that person or that institution in whose name executive acts are performed and the political society is represented on its external side (*e.g.*, by ambassadors). In Great Britain this is, at present, " Queen Victoria "; in France it is "The French Republic "; in a federal government it is, in federal matters, *e.g.*, " The United States of America," in matters of State sovereignty,

"The Commonwealth of Massachussetts," etc. By (2) the
legal sovereign, I mean, "as aforesaid," the sovereign for
the lawyer *quâ* lawyer. In Great Britain this is "as aforesaid" what lawyers mean by Parliament. (To the historian
the king is not a part of Parliament). In the United
States of America (I speak under correction of American
publicists) this is not Congress (as some Englishmen are apt
to think), nor the aggregate body of persons empowered to
amend the Constitution (as Austin thinks), but the written
Constitution itself, which, as it provides for the method of
its own amendment, and even limits the extent to which it
can be amended (Art. V.), is *legally* supreme over the determinate persons whom it entrusts with the power of amending
it. Thus the *legal* sovereign is not necessarily everywhere a
determinate body of persons any more than the *nominal*
sovereign; and (3) the ultimate *political* sovereign, *i.e.*,
public opinion or the "general will," never can be a determinate body of persons. It works through persons, of
course, but it is something vaguer and more powerful than
they.

The attempt to find sovereignty always and everywhere
in determinate persons is the great error of Austin. On
the other hand, the Austinians have done good service
by insisting on the legal irresponsibility of the legal
sovereign. Legal irresponsibility makes moral and political
responsibility the more conspicuous. If we know definitely
what the law is, we can more easily make up our minds
whether it is *politically* a good law or not. The ultimate
responsibility of the ultimate political sovereign is a question for the philosophy of history; in other words, one may

say it is a matter of "natural selection." The penalty for a continued mistaken exercise of the supreme power of public opinion is the penalty of death for the nation.

This whole subject of sovereignty I have attempted to treat more fully in an article which appears in the *Annals of the American Academy of Political and Social Science*, Vol. I., No. 3, and has been reprinted, with corrections, in *Darwin and Hegel, with other Philosophical Studies* (1893).

NOTE C.

UTILITARIANISM.

THROUGHOUT the foregoing Essays I have insisted that the question of the proper limits of State action must be determined, not by an *à priori* theory of "natural rights," nor by any respect for a supposed "sphere of individual freedom," with which we can say *beforehand* that the State has nothing whatever to do, nor by any quasi-scientific dogma about society being a natural growth with which it is foolish to meddle; but simply and entirely by "Utilitarian" considerations. This solution might indeed seem to plunge us into ethical controversies, and that might appear a bad way out of political difficulties. Ultimately, it is true, our ethical theories and our political practice must harmonise. But we may avoid the details of philosophical disputes. I have already indicated in what sense Utilitarianism is to be accepted as the determining principle for State action (See especially pages 107, 143). J. S. Mill, in his *Utilitarianism*, has practically deserted the Hedonism of Bentham by distinguishing pleasures according to kind; for this implies that some other criterion than that of pleasure determines moral quality. Here, as in so many other respects, Mill makes the beginning of a transition (Cp. p. 83 above). A theory of Utilitarianism based on Hedonism raises many questions which it cannot answer. Is it true that all sentient beings do always pursue pleasure? Is not "Happiness" something different from pleasure—something more, even, than pleasure *and* the absence of pain? How can we jump from "Every sentient being naturally pursues his own pleasure" (supposing it were true) to "Every one ought to seek the happiness of others"? I may assume that the negative criticism of Hedonism has done its work sufficiently; and it is superfluous to kill the dead. The critic does more important service when he points out that the cause of Bentham's errors lies in his abstract and mechanical view of feelings as if "lots of pleasures" could actually be distributed among the members of a community, like the dividends of a joint-stock company; and in his abstract and mechanical view of society, as if it were simply an aggregate of absolutely uniform individuals. A more adequate theory of the relation between the individual and society has been reached both by those (like T. H. Green), who, starting from the metaphysical conception of the "self," see that the self can only be realised in a society of other "selves," and by those (like Mr. Leslie Stephen) who apply the conception of Evolution to morality. (I can hardly take Mr. Spencer as an illustration, because, as already shown in other matters, his Evolutionism is half-hearted and vitiated by individualism). This "convergence of results," on the part of those who have approached the subject from different sides, is one of the most hopeful signs in the present revived interest in Ethics. (See an interesting passage in Mr. S. Alexander's *Moral Order and Progress*, pp. 6, 7).

Only "Intuitionism," and that in a mitigated form, remains as a survival of the older individualist theory. Intuitionist and evolutionist ethics are irreconcilable ; they both profess to be theories of the *origin* of moral ideas. On the other hand, I do not think there is anything ultimately inconsistent between a historical theory, which traces morality to the struggle for existence between societies, and a philosophical analysis, which shows that morality in its developed form implies the working of a self-consciousness which is not itself a mere part of nature. How exactly the two theories are to be adjusted I cannot consider here. In *Darwinism and Politics* (Edit. 2, pp. 104–106), I have said a little about the relation between Utilitarianism and the theory of Natural Selection. The conception of right conduct as conduct which tends to the welfare of the social organism avoids the defects of earlier Utilitarianism. On the other hand, Utilitarianism is a useful corrective to the fatalism that is apt to be the outcome of the first discovery that human society can be studied scientifically as well as the phenomena of nature. Utilitarianism lays stress on the deliberate adoption of the common good as the end of action. And when once we know something of the laws of social health and disease, we are surely better able to remedy the evils of society than before.

One great service that Evolutionist Utilitarianism is rendering to practical morality is the re-establishment of the connection between Ethics and Politics. We have come again to recognise, with Aristotle, the moral function of the State. We no longer draw a hard and fast line between the political and the moral, because we have found that we cannot draw a line at all, except for convenience of language, between society (which is not a mere aggregate, but an organism) and the individual (who is not a mere unit, but the member of an organism). We must not mistake abstractions for realities. So, too, in politics, it may be convenient, as a matter of statement, to separate off questions about the structure of the State from questions about its functions ; but for practical purposes such a separation is very misleading. Men may profess indifference about the form of government in comparison with the end or purpose of government ; but what the government *is* makes all the difference in determining what the government may safely be empowered to *do*. As we have seen, the distrust of all government action in general is, to a great extent, a false inference from the perfectly justifiable distrust of any action at all on the part of certain kinds of government. On the other hand, a recognition of what human society may do for itself by means of rational legislation enormously increases the importance of constitutional reform, which the· social reformer is too apt to thrust aside as merely "political." Merely political change, if that means change which has no social or moral purpose, is only possible to those who do not know, or do not believe in what they are doing. Machines are invented to do work ; and the kind of machine may make a great difference in the kind of work done.

Secondly, Utilitarianism has done something to restore another good element in Greek ethics, viz., the importance of knowledge. Bentham's saying, " Vice is miscalculation," is a somewhat mean-looking version of the Socratic doctrine that vice is ignorance. The importance of doing what we think right is generally insisted on ; but the importance of knowing what is right to do is apt to be disregarded. It is well to act up to our lights ; but how if our light be as darkness ? Intuitionist theories supposed every man to have " an infallible Pope in his own breast." The Utilitarian insists that the consequences of actions must be considered before we decide whether they are right or not. Accepted rules need revision and correction, not of course in the moment when they have to be applied—the battlefield is not the place for examining bayonets, though it certainly does test them. The conscience of the average man is apt to reflect the principles which belong to a social system that is passing away ; and, in any case, it is well that any principle or system which claims our obedience should have to face the question : Does it make for the common good or does it not ?

" The theory of Utility," says Sir H. Maine (*Early History of Institutions,* p. 399) " presupposes the theory of Equality." And, therefore, it is sometimes objected to Utilitarianism in ethics and politics that it rests ultimately on a metaphysical dogma. This has, indeed, often been the case : Equality has been assumed as a deduction from abstract justice. But a thorough-going Utilitarian must not shrink from applying the criterion of utility to the principle of Equality. If any one sincerely believes now-a-days that inequality promotes human well-being, and if he can discover any workable scheme for a society regulated by exact principles of geometrical proportion, he will have solved the problem that has baffled all legislators outside Plato's ideal

state. Most persons likely to take a Utilitarian point of
view would be willing to admit that to get rid of inequality
in social relations would be to get rid of one of the chief
sources of unhappiness in the world ; inequality is only
pleasing to despotic and to servile natures—I mean, of
course, permanent inequality, not the necessary temporary
inequalities for special purposes required by all orderly
work.   It is easy enough to point out that men are not
equal " by nature," *i.e.*, apart from the institutions of society.
But we have given up the doctrine of " natural rights,"
except as a statement of what we think *ought* to be.   And
when equality is claimed, it is put forward not as a fact, but as
an ideal, and must be defended on the ground of its utility
for social well-being.   Even Rousseau saw that the tendency of nature was to produce, not equality, but inequality ;
but for that very reason he held that the State ought to
endeavour to diminish, instead of (as has too often been
the case) exaggerating the inequalities of nature : " C'est
précisément parce que la force des choses tend toujours à
détruire l'égalité, que la force de la législation doit toujours
tendre à la maintenir." (*Contr. Soc.* II. 11.)   To put the
case for Equality on its lowest grounds, it is simply a rough
way of escaping the enormous difficulties of adjusting work
and reward in any way that will satisfy everybody.   To
put it on its highest grounds, true friendship, as Aristotle
saw, is only possible between equals, or those who will treat
each other as equals.   Only in a society of equals who are,
as it were, his " other selves," can an individual realise the
best life possible for himself.